Hitler in History

D1455564

The Tauber Institute for the Study of European Jewry, established by a gift to Brandeis University by Dr. Laszlo N. Tauber, is dedicated to the memory of the victims of Nazi persecutions between 1933 and 1945. The Institute seeks to study the history and culture of European Jewry in the modern period. The Institute has a special interest in studying the causes, nature and consequences of the European Jewish catastrophe and seeks to explore them within the context of modern European diplomatic, intellectual, political and social history. The Tauber Institute for the Study of European Jewry is organized on a multi-disciplinary basis with the participation of scholars in history, Judaic studies, political science, sociology, comparative literature and other disciplines.

PUBLISHED FOR BRANDEIS UNIVERSITY PRESS
BY UNIVERSITY PRESS OF NEW ENGLAND
Hanover and London

Hitler in History

EBERHARD JÄCKEL

UNIVERSITY PRESS OF NEW ENGLAND

BRANDEIS UNIVERSITY

BROWN UNIVERSITY

CLARK UNIVERSITY

UNIVERSITY OF CONNECTICUT

DARTMOUTH COLLEGE

UNIVERSITY OF NEW HAMPSHIRE

UNIVERSITY OF RHODE ISLAND

TUFTS UNIVERSITY

UNIVERSITY OF VERMONT

Copyright 1984 by Eberhard Jäckel

All rights reserved. Except for brief quotation in critical articles or reviews, this book, or parts thereof,
must not be reproduced in any form without permis-
sion in writing from the publisher. For further information contact University Press of New England,
Hanover, NH 03755.

Printed in the United States of America

Library of Congress Cataloging in Publication Data
Jäckel, Eberhard.
    Hitler in history.
    Series from the Tauber Institute for the Study of European Jewry; 3)
    Bibliography: p.   Includes index.
        1. Hitler, Adolf, 1889–1945. 2. Germany—Politics and
government—1918–1933. 3. Germany—Politics and
government—1933–1945. 4. World War, 1939–1945.
5. Holocaust, Jewish (1939–1945) 6. Heads of state—
Germany—Biography. 1. Title. 11. Series.
    DD247.H5J29 1984   943.086'092'4 [B]   84-40304
    ISBN 0-87451-311-1 (cloth)
    ISBN 0-87451-502-5 (paper)

5   4   3

Contents

Preface

The man whose name appears in the title of this book and in the headings of each of its chapters has determined my life to a degree that embarrasses me. I was three and a half when he came to power and almost sixteen when he killed himself. I grew up under him, went to his schools, lived through his war. Only after he disappeared, though, did I feel his full impact upon me. Among my first postwar readings were reports on his camps and on the Nuremberg trials. I realized that I had lived under a criminal. I began to wonder then how his rule had come about, and in the country in which I had been born. It was largely with these questions in mind that I took up the study of history.

I read his book, for the first time, in that winter of 1945 without understanding it, but on rereading it several years later I suddenly discovered that he had set down in the 1920s what he would do in the 1940s. Above all, his two goals, a war of conquest and the elimination of the Jews, were clearly stated. I had been told that he was a lunatic, but I found that he had at least been consistent. I chose that topic when I became a professor and had to deliver an inaugural lecture. A publisher sitting in the audience suggested that I write a small book on it. This came out in 1969. It was criticized by some for not explaining how such a man could have come to power and put his ideas into practice. That had not been my subject, but it was the very question that had intrigued me since 1945.

When I was invited to deliver a series of lectures at the Tauber Institute at Brandeis University in September and October 1983 I took the opportunity to assemble the answers I had found over the years. The views presented here are thus the result of several years of work. The first chapter offers an explanation of how such a man came to power. The next two are corollaries of the two central chapters of my earlier book. There I had attempted to show how that man had formulated his goals; here I have tried to explain how he implemented them. The fourth examines why he declared war on the United States. The last chapter was not delivered as a lecture at Brandeis, but rather was added to the second German edition of my earlier book. Since the chapter did not appear in the English translation, I decided to include it here. The chapter introduces some additional considerations while also summarizing my research and conclusions. It has been translated by Maria Tatar, to whom I am indebted for her excellent work.

I am pleased to express my gratitude once more to the Tauber Institute and its former director, Professor Bernard Wasserstein, for their invitation. I also wish to thank my listeners again for their patience with my lectures and for their challenging questions that followed. My greatest thanks go to my friend Rudolph Binion. Not only were these lectures originally proposed by him. If they have attained a measure of readability it is because of his painstaking corrections and revisions of my English. I appreciate his labors all the more as he disagrees with me on many points. The least I can do is stress that the polish is his and the shortcomings mine. I should like to include Roberta Recht in my thanks. Rudy's and her kindness made my weeks at Brandeis an unforgettable pleasure.

Stuttgart, December 1983

Hitler in History

1
Hitler Comes to Power

For all those interested in German history, and perhaps not for them alone, the seminal question of the twentieth century is: How could Hitler come to power? The question has been raised many times and has received almost as many answers. Yet Hitler's accession to power on January 30, 1933, one of the crucial events of our century, seems to be obscured rather than explained by the very mass of information and by the innumerable interpretations concerned with it. We know much, but we understand little about how Germany came to give itself over to a dictatorship that turned out to be of unprecedented criminality in history. It might be refreshing, therefore, just to apply the known facts to simple questions and answers. Let us avoid sweeping statements and instead ask modest but precise questions without hesitating to repeat the obvious. We shall begin with unquestionable facts and try to explain them as precisely as possible in the light of our present knowledge.

The first fact is that Hitler came to power as chancellor because President Hindenburg appointed him. That is indis-

putable. It was in the first instance not groups such as industry, or systems like capitalism, or authoritarian ideas, that
brought the leader of the Nazi party to power; it was simply
the president. Again, Hitler did not come to power through a
coup d'état or a revolution, but rather by appointment within
the constitutional framework of the Weimar Republic.

The first question, therefore, is a double one: Why did
Hindenburg appoint Hitler, and how was he able to do so?
For human beings do not act only from personal motives.
They act also, and above all, according to certain conditions.
They cannot do everything they want to do. Of what they
want to do, they do only what they can. We shall therefore
analyze primarily, not Hindenburg's motives, but the condi-
tions under which he acted.

We may anticipate a simple answer: Hindenburg appointed
Hitler because Hitler was the leader of the strongest party in
Germany. This statement remains to be elaborated but it will
be found to be as indisputable as the first one. The next
question will then have to be why and how the Nazi party had
become the strongest party.

One objection can be raised against the assumptions im-
plied in the second question just posed. The Nazi party had
already become the strongest party six months earlier, during
the elections of July 31, 1932. Consequently we must ask
why Hitler was not appointed chancellor until half a year
later. Again we can anticipate a simple answer: The Nazis did
not have a majority in the Reichstag either in the summer of
1932 or at the time of Hitler's appointment. Hitler was not
brought to power by a parliamentary majority; nearly two
thirds of the German electorate had not voted for him. This
fact complicates our understanding of the events. Had the
Nazi party held a majority in the Reichstag, the appointment
of Hitler would be easier to explain. We would have to ask
only how that majority had come about. Nevertheless, although the Nazis did not have a majority, their limited elec-

toral successes are one condition that led to Hitler's appointment as chancellor. This leads us to our third question: Why
and how did this party come into being? This question must
be clearly separated from that regarding the party's electoral
successes. For the successes began only after 1929, whereas
the party was founded in 1919.

Thus we have arrived at the triple question. It concerns first
of all Hindenburg, who appointed Hitler; second, the voters
who made Hitler a political factor; and third, the party that
attracted the voters. All three questions have to be raised
together. Whoever asks only about Hindenburg neglects the
electorate, without which he would not have appointed Hitler.
Again, whoever asks only about the electorate overlooks the
fact that it did not give the Nazi party a majority. And whoever asks only about the party needs reminding that it would
not have come to power without the electorate and without
Hindenburg. Let us begin, therefore, at the logical beginning,
with the question why Hindenburg appointed Hitler.

THE ROLE OF HINDENBURG

Although in appointing Hitler chancellor Hindenburg acted
within the framework of the constitution, he was not required
to appoint him at any time. Article 53 of the Weimar constitution empowered the president to appoint the chancellor of his
choice.[1] This freedom was restricted only by Article 54, which
stipulated that the chancellor and the ministers must command the confidence of the Reichstag.

Thus, Hitler or any would-be chancellor could not simply
concern himself with his own appointment; he needed the
backing of a majority in the Reichstag. This meant 293 votes
of the then 584 members. The Nazis numbered only 196.
They were 97 seats short of a majority, thus Hitler formed
a coalition cabinet. His coalition partner, the Conservative
party, however, had only 52 members in parliament, leav-

ing the Hitler government short 45 seats for an absolute majority. Thus Hitler's government, like its three predecessors, was a so-called presidential cabinet.

A presidential cabinet was not provided for in the constitution, but had a legal basis in it through a combination of Articles 48 and 53. According to Article 48 the president could take any steps necessary to restore law and order should they be considerably disturbed or endangered. The president alone decided when that state of emergency had been reached and what measures could be taken. The constitution called for a law to provide detailed regulations for carrying out Article 48, but such a law was never passed. The president's power under Article 48 was restricted, however, by the stipulation that he inform the Reichstag immediately of any emergency measures taken; the Reichstag could in turn annul those measures by a simple majority vote. Thus the president's immense emergency powers could be nullified if and when the majority of the members of parliament so wished.

It was on this legal basis that Germany had been governed since March 30, 1930. Pursuant to Article 53 of the Weimar constitution the president had appointed three successive chancellors: Heinrich Brüning, Franz von Papen, and Kurt von Schleicher. None of them commanded the confidence of the Reichstag. But since the Reichstag's confidence did not need to be overtly expressed, only overtly denied, the chancellors governed so long as a vote of no confidence was not put. They governed with the backing, or confidence, of the president alone.

Laws were a different matter. The laws had to be passed by the Reichstag. If laws were needed and their passage was not likely, the president might issue decrees under Article 48 without having to justify his initiative by proving that public order was considerably disturbed or endangered. These decrees, which were called emergency decrees, did not have to be passed by the Reichstag. But, again, the Reichstag could annul them by a simple majority vote. If this happened, the government could no longer govern. Brüning's cabinet faced this challenge on July 18, 1930.

In this circumstance the president had still another weapon. According to Article 25 he could dissolve the Reichstag. Within sixty days of a dissolution a general election had to be held. Hindenburg dissolved the Reichstag on July 18, 1930, and made full use of the period of sixty days that followed. During this time his chancellor could continue to govern without fear of interference from the Reichstag. When the Reichstag reassembled after the election of September 14, however, the government found that its support in the parliament had decreased. Yet it was precisely because of the erosion of his support through the Nazi victory of September 14, 1930, that Brüning was able to remain in office for another eighteen months. In order to prevent Brüning's fall and Hitler's possible accession to the chancellorship, the majority of the Reichstag no longer used its right to put a vote of no confidence or to annul Brüning's numerous emergency decrees. The Reichstag was prepared to tolerate the chancellor. Brüning was finally dismissed by Hindenburg on May 30, 1932, and was succeeded by Papen. For the time being we shall not deal with the reasons for Brüning's dismissal or with the political and economic issues behind these developments, but shall continue merely to explain their constitutional implications.

Unlike Brüning's cabinet, Papen's ultraconservative cabinet could not expect to be tolerated by the Reichstag, and the Reichstag was again dissolved immediately after Papen was appointed. This gave him the chance of governing freely for fifty-seven days, until the election of July 31. He won another month's reprieve because the Reichstag was not bound to assemble until thirty days after the election, according to Article 23. When the Reichstag finally convened on August 30, it passed a vote of no confidence against Papen by the enormous majority of 512 voted against 42 with 5 abstentions.

This should have meant that the chancellor was deposed, but either immediately before or after this vote (a question that remained unresolved in the tumultuous session) the Reichstag was dissolved once more and Papen again gained fifty-five days, until the election of November 6. But this election also failed to produce a working majority; Papen had thus failed in his attempts to form a government with majority support. On December 6, thirty days after the election, the new Reichstag would reassemble and Papen could expect another vote of no confidence, after which not even Hindenburg could save him.

Hindenburg now had three options. He could immediately dissolve the Reichstag again. Papen would then have gained another three months in office—sixty days until the election and another thirty until the reassembly of the Reichstag. But this method was outworn and on the brink of illegality, and it did not promise a way out of the crisis.

Second, Hindenburg could accept Papen's suggestion to dissolve the Reichstag but delay the election beyond the prescribed day. This would have been a blatant breach of the constitution, and Hindenburg was not prepared to do this. He would have to break his oath to the constitution, which he took seriously, and he would have to answer to the supreme court, a circumstance that would have rendered the country altogether ungovernable. He could also have prompted a civil war, which the army declared itself incapable of winning for several reasons, including the possibility that other countries such as Poland might exploit the internal strife in Germany.

There remained only a third option: to appoint a new chancellor. Hence Papen was dismissed and on December 2, 1932, four days before the new Reichstag was to assemble, Schleicher was appointed. The Reichstag restrained itself from passing an immediate vote of no confidence against the new chancellor. It adjourned until after Christmas and Schleicher gained a brief respite to govern.

Sooner or later, as Schleicher knew, the responsible committee would summon the Reichstag again. After a second postponement the committee set the date of Tuesday, January 31, 1933. Schleicher had failed to rally a majority, and Hindenburg was again confronted with the same three options he had faced in November. Again he rejected a breach of the constitution, which Schleicher now suggested to him. In the end he even denied Schleicher the constitutional recourse of dissolving the Reichstag, whereupon the chancellor resigned on Saturday, January 28.

On Monday, January 30, Hindenburg appointed Hitler. We are now able to understand better the advantages that this move held for the president. As we have seen, Hitler also lacked a majority in parliament, but together with his Conservative partners he was short only forty-five votes. This was a much broader parliamentary basis for governing than either Papen or Schleicher had had. If the Reichstag were dissolved now (as it was soon after), it could be hoped that the new coalition government would win the necessary forty-five seats and so attain a majority in parliament. Thus it would be possible to restore the original sense of the constitution.

This sounds altogether cynical and holds true in a purely formalistic sense only, since Hitler was a declared enemy of the constitution and had never hidden his intention of abolishing it. But Hitler promised to abolish the constitution without breaching it. He proposed to use constitutional means to gain a parliamentary majority in order to destroy the constitution by due process. This was in accordance with Hindenburg's wishes. Hindenburg was not a democrat but basically a royalist. He did not want to preserve the constitution at all costs. He only wanted to avoid breaching it and, formally speaking, he was successful. We may say, therefore, that Hindenburg appointed Hitler because Hitler offered an opportunity to render the country governable again without breaching the constitution.

Needless to say, this explanation is not yet sufficient. It covers only a superficial series of events, and we need to know more, for example, about Hindenburg's motives. We can say at once that he was not pleased by his appointment of Hitler. Hitler was not his favorite candidate . Personally and politically Brüning and Papen had been to his liking; Hitler was not. Hindenburg despised this Bohemian corporal, as he called him, and recognized the potential dangers of his accession with remarkable insight. Moreover they had been opposing candidates in a bitter presidential election in the spring of 1932.

On November 24, 1932, Hindenburg had informed Hitler that he could not appoint him chancellor because he feared that "a presidential cabinet led by Hitler would necessarily develop into a party dictatorship with all its consequences for an extreme aggravation of the conflicts within the German people." As late as January 26, 1933, Hindenburg told his entourage: "Gentlemen, I hope you will not hold me capable of appointing this Austrian corporal to be Reich chancellor." And it was with an expression of resignation that on January 28 he asked his advisers who had opened the way to a Hitler government, "Does this mean that I have the unpleasant task of appointing this Hitler chancellor?" [2]

To understand how Hindenburg overcame his distaste for and doubts about Hitler, we must examine once more the conditions under which he acted at the end of 1932 and beginning of 1933. The president's freedom to act was considerable but not unlimited. The Reichstag could in principle at any time have proposed a candidate who commanded a majority and Hindenburg would in all likelihood have appointed him chancellor. He could appoint chancellors of his own choice only because the Reichstag itself no longer presented any majority candidate. On the other hand, Hindenburg's minority chancellors could govern only as long as they were at least tolerated by the Reichstag. This had not been the case since the dismissal of Brüning.

By dismissing Brüning needlessly in May 1932, Hindenburg created the predicament that ultimately led him to appoint Hitler. Hindenburg dismissed Brüning because the president wanted to move away from the parliamentary regime and gradually introduce a more conservative and authoritarian system that might eventually lead to the restoration of the monarchy. We can go further and say that the same intentions guided him when he appointed Brüning. In itself this does not require much of an explanation. The old field marshal was, we repeat, not a democrat but a royalist. What requires an explanation is not his lifelong royalist convictions but the conditions under which he could implement them. This, in turn, raises questions about the basic structural problems of the Weimar Republic.

No political party in the Weimar Republic had ever had an absolute majority; hence all the governments were coalitions and most of them had only minority support in the Reichstag. The first duly constituted German government after the fall of the empire in November 1918 and the national elections of 1919 consisted of Social Democrats, left Liberals, and Catholic Centrists. This so-called Weimar coalition, which then drew up the Weimar constitution, lost its majority in the election of 1920 and never regained it. These three parties were basically the only ones firmly tied to the Weimar constitution, although there are some reservations in the case of the Center party. We can say, therefore, that the parliamentary, democratic, and republican form of government had had no support from the majority of the population since 1920.

Another group of parties, led by the Conservatives and the right Liberals, adhered to the idea of a constitutional monarchy, like the one that had ruled Germany until November 1918. But these parties also failed to win a majority. They could govern only in partnership with at least one party from the Weimar coalition.

The situation in the Weimar Republic in the 1920s had reached a stalemate. Neither of the two leading groups in German society was strong enough to govern the state alone, but each was strong enough to prevent the other from doing so. Since their differences stemmed from their principles, compromises were difficult. They recognized no common ground on which they could explain and settle normal conflicting interests. The stalemate, with its roots deep in German history, came to a head after the First World War. The Conservatives scored a victory in 1925 when Hindenburg was elected president. The Republicans, in turn, scored a victory in 1928 when they almost regained the majority in the Reichstag and a Social Democrat became chancellor once again.

None of these victories was decisive or broke the stalemate. But the Conservatives were alarmed at the success of the Left in 1928 and thereupon tried, with the help of the president, to regain the position they had held until 1918. Their chance came in March 1930 when the Social Democratic chancellor Hermann Müller and, with him, the last majority government of the Weimar Republic resigned.[3] Hindenburg seized this opportunity to become independent of parliamentary majorities and to appoint Brüning. If we say that the downhill course that led to Hitler's appointment in January 1933 began with Brüning's appointment in March 1930, then we can also say that Hindenburg's undemocratic attitude contributed strongly to this development. Had Hindenburg been a convinced supporter of the parliamentary system of government he would have negotiated another majority government. Since he was not a supporter but an opponent of the parliamentary system, and since he particularly disliked the Social Democrats, he snatched the opportunity to get rid of them when it arose in March 1930.

It is equally true that Hindenburg was able to appoint Brüning and the other, later minority, chancellors only because by March 1930 the Reichstag itself was no longer able to form a majority government. Had a majority chancellor been proposed, Hindenburg would most likely have appointed him and let him govern. He never envisaged a coup d'état or wished Hitler to come to power. He only sought to profit from the given situation, from what we have described as a stalemate. Today we know that the Müller cabinet, had it not broken up, could have survived the worst part of the international economic crisis with a sound parliamentary majority, since its legislative term did not expire until May 1932. Instead, the Reichstag was prematurely dissolved and in the elections of September 1930 Hitler won his first major break-through.

This is worth repeating. The Müller cabinet was not overthrown in March 1930; it resigned. It is well known that the coalition partners could not agree on a question of unemployment benefits. But to see this as the reason for the resignation of the cabinet would be to confuse the long-term cause with the immediate trigger. The crucial factor was the structural stalemate of the Weimar Republic. Under the conditions of a stalemate Hindenburg was able to appoint his conservative minority chancellors. When they were no longer tolerated by the Reichstag, the state became ungovernable. In the course of the periodic elections held in hopes of providing these minority chancellors with a majority, the Nazi party became instead the strongest party. Still Hindenburg refused to appoint Hitler after these elections; he declined explicitly in August 1931 and again in November 1932.

We have to ask, therefore, why he changed his mind in January 1933. The answer is clear. The Conservative party in the meantime had been persuaded to form a coalition with the Nazi party and Hitler had reduced his demands. Apart from himself, only two Nazis were to become members of the cabinet; in addition, two ministers belonged to the Conservative party, and the rest were independents. Hindenburg's adviser, Papen, became vice chancellor. Finally, before appointing Hitler, Hindenburg had been allowed to appoint a defense minister of his own choice. In other words, the risks involved in Hitler's appointment had been reduced for Hindenburg. Hitler had been "fenced in," as the famous formula ran, and with that, Hindenburg's doubts had been appeased.

The distribution of authority in the new coalition government was the result of unusual negotiations. Normally the president directed such negotiations himself (he did so for the last time in November 1932), since he was the one who finally had to appoint the chancellor. Hitler was the first and only chancellor whom Hindenburg appointed without having negotiated with him beforehand. Instead, the negotiations had been conducted by Papen, who managed to create the coalition that was formed on January 30. It was above all Papen who had allayed Hindenburg's doubts.

Papen's role is well known. He was not a member of parliament, not even a member of a political party, let alone the leader of one (he had once played a minor role in the Center party). Nor was he the delegated leader of any organized group. He was a private person, accountable to no one, free of all responsibilities, indeed irresponsible in every sense. His power rested solely on Hindenburg's trust, which he had gained when he was chancellor. The fact that as a former chancellor he was pressing for his own return to power is obvious and can be accepted without further elaboration. The additional consideration that Papen was shortsighted and frivolous is perhaps relevant but beyond the scope of our historical inquiry. The one point that does have to be recognized is that he was in a position to direct the vital negotiations in a national crisis. The responsibility for forming a cabinet had passed first from the parties to the president and then from the president to a private person.

As far as Papen's negotiations are concerned, we neither can nor need to describe their complicated course here. All we need to know is that the industrialist Wilhelm Keppler, who was also Hitler's economic adviser, had persuaded a banker, Kurt von Schröder, to arrange a meeting between Hitler and Papen, which took place at Schröder's house in Cologne on January 4, 1933. As a result of this and many subsequent consultations, Papen and others persuaded Hindenburg to appoint Hitler.

This series of meetings raises the question of the role of industry in Hitler's accession.[4] We will examine this highly controversial issue with particular care by extracting the real questions from the morass of sweeping statements that usually accompany them. It is obvious that the general statement that Hitler was brought to power by industry or industrialists is of no use. Neither is it helpful to demonstrate that any number of industrialists recommended Hitler's coming to power or promoted it in other ways. Our task is rather to see whether this support did in fact contribute to Hitler's coming to power. Various answers to this question are possible. The first could be that industrialists induced Papen to negotiate with Hitler. This is improbable. Immediately after his dismissal Papen began trying to form a new government; his desire to return to power is a sufficient explanation for this. Nevertheless, Papen's access to Hitler remains a problem. The two men were not on good terms, which may explain why Papen needed mediators, but these could have been lawyers as well as industrialists. Even if we assume that the mediators had a strong influence on the negotiations, the decision to appoint Hitler after the negotiations lay with Hindenburg alone.

The second and more important question, therefore, is

whether representatives of industry and finance persuaded Hindenburg to appoint Hitler. Such attempts were doubtless made. In November 1932 leading industrial representatives had asked Hindenburg in a letter to appoint Hitler head of a presidential cabinet. But it is most unlikely that such initiatives influenced Hindenburg's decision. Hindenburg despised industrialists and bankers and disliked following their advice. There were no industrialists in his political or personal entourage. Rather, his advisers were civil servants and army officers, his friends were landowners. The latter were especially influential at the end. The landowners opposed Schleicher because he wanted to cut the subvention of public money for the indebted landholders of East Elbia. There is plenty of evidence for this, and if Hindenburg was at all influenced in his decision making by the promptings of special interest groups, then it was by landed rather than by industrial interests. In saying this, we do not, however, intend to assign to landed interests the role that industry plays in various other explanations.

Another possibility in defining the role played by industry is that it paid Hitler and thus helped him to become a powerful political factor. We will postpone this question until we consider Hitler's electoral successes.

Let us return to the question how Papen came to conduct the negotiations for the formation of the government. The first factor was Hindenburg's confidence in him. Another precondition was the fact that the state apparatus had become largely autonomous. Here I shall follow Karl Marx in differentiating between state power and state apparatus. State power is the ability to pass laws and directives, which are then executed by the state apparatus. This state apparatus consists of the civil service, the judiciary, the army, and the police. All of them are subject to directives. Generally speaking, the state power is exercised by the ruling classes or, in a democracy, by those who are elected by the majority of the population. They then direct the state apparatus by giving it instructions. If the state power, however, is not clearly exercised by one group, or if the population cannot agree on whom to entrust with the state power, then that state apparatus becomes more or less free from directives, more or less independent. This became increasingly the case in the Weimar Republic.

One particularly clear example of this is Kurt von Schleicher's political role. Originally an army officer, later a leading official in the Ministry of Defense, Schleicher gained influence because the political parties left him without instructions. Although it was not his job, in 1932 he recommended to Hindenburg that Papen be appointed Chancellor, thus providing Papen with the influential position that later enabled him to form the Hitler cabinet.

Schleicher and Papen were not party representatives. Schleicher belonged to the state apparatus; Papen was, as we have said, a private person with no party affiliation. The normal party competition for state power had been replaced by personal rivalries and intrigues. Even the position of the president had become independent. He had, of course, gained a share of state power by being elected. But this part was normally checked by parliament, which held another and larger share of state power. It was parliament that had the authority to determine which government the president was to appoint. By resigning this right, parliament shifted its share of state power to the president. Hindenburg had not competed for this share; it had fallen into his lap. Consequently, he had more or less the entire state power at his disposal. He in turn handed it over in large measure to the state apparatus. Thus the people around Hindenburg were able to increase their power. This was the case not only with Schleicher and Papen but also with Otto Meissner, the president's secretary of state, with other civil servants, and with Oskar, the president's son, who as a cynic remarked had not been provided for in the constitution.

None of Hindenburg's advisers or confidants was a Nazi; none wanted Hitler to come to power. They had profited from the situation as it had arisen and were free to steer a course of conservative reaction. But this course failed under conditions of economic crisis and rendered the state ungovernable. Then, confronted with chaos and fearing a communist revolution, Hindenburg and his associates saw no other way out of the crisis that they had to a great extent produced than to recommend Hitler, who had become a powerful factor as a result of that crisis and the electorate's response to it.

THE VOTER SUPPORT FOR HITLER

When we consider the electoral success of the Nazi party, we must remember that the Nazis had been a splinter party until 1929. During the Reichstag elections of 1924 they had been banned, Hitler was still in prison, and the substitute organization won 3.0 percent of the votes. In the Reichstag elections of 1928 this percentage dropped to 2.6. Under normal procedures this Nazi representation in parliament would not have changed until 1932, but Brüning's failure in July 1930 meant new elections. Hitler's breakthrough on the national level, after limited success in local and regional elections, came during the election of September 1930. The number of Nazi votes rose from 800,000 to 6.4 million, their proportion of the total from 2.6 to 18.3 percent, the number of Nazi seats from 12 to 107. This was the greatest increase ever gained by a party from one election to the next in German history. This trend continued in the elections to provincial diets in 1931. It reached its peak in Oldenburg, where the Nazi party gained 37.2 percent of the votes.

In 1932 five major elections were held, two for the office of president, two for the renewal of the Reichstag, and one to the Prussian diet. Hitler won 31.1 percent of the votes on the first ballot of the presidential election on March 13 and 36.8 percent on the second ballot on April 10. A fortnight later the Nazis won 36.6 percent in the Prussian election. They reached 37.3 percent in the Reichstag election on July 31; this was the largest percentage the Nazis ever won in free elections. Compared with the results of the previous Reichstag election, their gains had more than doubled and thus set another record. The number of Nazi seats in parliament rose from 107 to 230, making the Nazi party the strongest parliamentary group. These gains were then followed by an extremely remarkable development. In the election held on November 6, 1932, the Nazi votes sank from 37.3 to 33.1 percent, the number of Nazi voters from 13.4 to 11.4 million, and the number of Nazi seats from 230 to 196. Even though the Nazis remained the strongest party, the decline was considerable. Two million people had either abandoned them or not voted at all. It was only after this electoral setback that Hitler's party came to power.

Before we try to explain these developments we should remind ourselves that any statement about the causes of an electoral shift is to a large extent guesswork. This is true even more for the Weimar Republic in the 1930s than for countries today, for election research was then still in its infancy and opinion polls did not yet exist.

In principle a shift of votes can be explained in one of two ways. First, we can ask which parties gained and which parties lost votes, assuming that the gainers drew votes from the losers. The big losers in 1930 were the right-wing non-Nazi parties, which in Germany were called the bourgeois parties (*bürgerliche Parteien*). They lost three million votes. One could, therefore, assume that a good half of the Nazi gains came from there, but this is unsatisfactory because the overall number of votes increased considerably between the two elections. In 1930 4.2 million more people voted than in 1928. Since the Nazis gained 5.6 million votes, the majority of these were not necessarily drawn from other parties. It might just as well have been largely former nonvoters or new, first-time voters who brought about Hitler's breakthrough.

The picture is somewhat clearer for 1932. In the July election the total number of votes rose by 1.9 million, while the Nazi votes rose by 7.4 million. This time, therefore, the bulk of the new Nazi votes must have come from the other parties. Once more the so-called bourgeois parties were the biggest losers, including some that had managed to hold their positions in 1930. Their losses amounted to 5.3 million votes altogether. If the 1.9 million new votes are added, we have a total of 7.2 million votes, which almost accounts for the entire 7.4 million additional Nazi votes. As far as the parties on the left are concerned, the Social Democrats lost 618,000 votes and the Communists gained 691,000. Although it cannot be ruled out that former supporters of the Social Democratic party went over to the Nazis, it is more likely that they switched to the Communist party. But again it can safely be concluded that the bulk of the new Nazi votes must have come from the so-called bourgeois parties.

A second way of explaining a shift of votes is by electoral geography: We consider the constituencies and polling areas in which the Nazis gained more than their average increase and then argue from the social structure of those areas to the social structure of the electorate. Research in this field is in a state of flux. Nevertheless, recent studies, particularly Richard F. Hamilton's excellent *Who Voted for Hitler?*, demonstrate again that it was the middle classes, the more well-to-do rather than workers or the unemployed, who voted for the Nazis.

Before considering the motives of the Nazi voters, we should investigate whether industry contributed to Hitler's electoral successes. It is quite clear from a quick look at the several millions of shifting votes that they cannot be explained by financial support from industry. So many votes just cannot be commandeered. Moreover, the Nazi party was not on good terms with industry. The industrialists' party was the German People's party, and in the presidential election of 1932 industry supported Hindenburg against Hitler. Industry saw its interests well represented by the Papen government. There is no doubt that after the Nazi party had become a powerful factor as a result of its electoral successes, industrial circles attempted to help it enter the government, recognizing that the party was both popular and antisocialist. But we have already expressed our doubts about whether these attempts had a great influence on Hindenburg.

In general, we can offer little more than guesses about the motives of the Nazi voters, but this does not mean our guesses must be random. The fact that the peak of the economic crisis and the peak of Nazi electoral success were simultaneous has always prompted the conclusion that there was a causal connection between the two. In fact there was, but not necessarily the one that has often been assumed. Previous analyses suggesting that the simultaneous increase in unemployment and Nazi votes meant that the unemployed tended to vote for Hitler have found no support in recent research. If on the other hand, as we have found, the Nazi voters belonged mostly to the propertied middle classes, then we must deal with a different set of motives. A more likely assumption is that the impoverished turned to the Communists or remained loyal to the Social Democrats, whereas those who voted for the Nazis were motivated not by actual impoverishment but by a fear of future misery.

This generalized fear may have included a fear of communism. It had definitely been the nightmare of the bourgeoisie, and not only in Germany, since 1917. Anticommunism was also a principal item of Hitler's public program. It is, furthermore, indisputable that the Communist party grew steadily. It was in fact the only party of this period that enjoyed an uninterrupted increase in the Reichstag vote. The party won 10.6 percent of the vote in May 1928, 13.1 percent in September 1930, 14.3 percent in July 1932, and 16.3 percent in November 1932. Unlike the Nazi party, the Communist party did not decline in November 1932. Moreover, it called for expropriation and promised Bolshevism, thus sowing panic among property owners. There is thus a strong basis for the suggestion that the economic crisis and the simultaneous rise of the Communist party drove many bourgeois voters into Hitler's arms. The people surrounding Hindenburg might have been motivated by the same fear, even though they did not favor the Nazis but rather suspected them of socialist tendencies. It is usually forgotten that in Hindenburg's eyes Hitler belonged to the left rather than to the right of the political spectrum.

Although the question of the social background of the Nazi voters and their motives is of great importance, it is not crucial to our main question—how Hitler came to power. The Nazi party was not a standard party that intended to represent the interests of its members and voters or those of certain social classes. Nor did it take these interests into account or formulate its political objectives according to specific class or group interests.

Rather the Nazi party was a movement whose followers let themselves be led by a charismatic figure without wanting to know exactly whether and how he would represent their interests. The party had no decision-making committees that passed plans of action. The party congresses were purely declamatory events. The party platform could not be changed after its proclamation in 1920. Since the führer was not elected after 1921, he was independent of any sort of organization, not subject to supervision, not answerable to anyone. He demanded and was given absolute obedience, and it is significant that his followers called themselves his retainers. The Nazi party was a movement of an almost religious character, with an uncontested leader at its head and obedient followers behind him. Hence its social structure is not of great importance. What is important is that its members never formulated their own political aims, but rather followed their leader in such increasing numbers that by 1932 he controlled the strongest party in Germany.

THE NAZI PARTY

Our analysis of Hitler's rise to power and the role of the voters forces us to look more closely at the Nazi party. How and why did this party come into being? This too is a complex problem. I shall restrict myself to a few points that are crucial for my argument.

The Nazi party, founded in 1919, was a product of the German defeat in World War I. This was true for the founders and again especially for the man who not only soon became the party leader but also made the party the basis for his career. Hitler was already thirty years old in 1919 and had not been previously interested in politics. That is unusual and supports the statement that he so often repeated, namely, that it was the German defeat in the war that led to his decision to become a politician.

In its ideology the Nazi party followed an older nationalist, anti-Semitic, and antisocialist tradition. Hitler used these components to formulate his own views, but these attracted little interest within the party and were almost completely passed over in silence after 1930. His supporters were held together by their common trust in their leader and his assurance that he would make up for the earlier defeat, punish those who were responsible for it, and lead the country back to its former greatness.

This brings us to the end of our first inquiry. Although we have posed simple questions, we have not found simple answers in the sense that Hitler's coming to power can be explained by one reason alone or that his rule was based on the support of one social class only. Actually, his rule was more or less independent of classes altogether. Such regimes are exceptional in history, but Hitler's was not the first of its kind. The basic condition for his coming to power was what we have described as a stalemate—the approximate deadlock of the leading classes.

If history is seen as a series of class struggles fought for the possession of state power, then it follows that occasionally old classes decline and new classes rise. Within this process there is bound to come a time when the chief declining and the chief rising class are of almost equal strength. Then neither of the two main competing classes is able to direct the state alone, whereas each one can prevent the other from doing so. This is always a critical moment. In French history it led, for example, to the accession of Napoleon I and later of Napoleon III. In German history a similar stage was reached in the first third of the twentieth century, beginning even before 1914. The parties of the Weimar coalition had held the majority in parliament as early as 1912. They lost that majority in 1920 and almost regained it in 1928. Thus the struggle was long and not decided by 1933.

This long-term struggle between competing but evenly matched parties was complicated in Germany by two short-term extraneous factors. The first of these factors was the collapse of Germany at the end of World War I, which produced the Nazi party. The second was the Great Depression, which promoted the electoral success of the Nazi party and its leader, who by that time had become a charismatic figure. At this point the state apparatus was handed over to this leader by certain individuals who had gained possession of it as a consequence of the long-term political struggles. They acted without instructions from but in the perceived interests of the declining class. They hoped to be able to use Hitler and to control him, but they failed. It was he who took control of the state apparatus and later the state power, to establish a regime of terror.

2

Hitler Wages War

Perhaps never in history did a ruler write down before he came to power what he was to do afterward as precisely as did Adolf Hitler. Hitler set himself two goals: a war of conquest and the elimination of the Jews. And it is well known that his rule was indeed marked by these two undertakings. In my book entitled *Hitler's World View* I dealt extensively with the formulation of these aims.[1] In this and the following chapter I shall concentrate instead on their implementation. In order to explain my approach, let me repeat one point from chapter 1. Human beings do not act only from personal motives. They act also, and above all, according to certain conditions. They cannot do everything they want to do. Of what they want to do, they do only what they can. We shall therefore analyze primarily, not Hitler's motives, but the conditions that enabled him to pursue his aims and the ways and means by which he did so.

We can formulate our inquiry in terms of two main questions. The first concerns the interior and the second the exterior conditions of Hitler's acts. The first question is, How was

Hitler able to acquire and maintain a position in Germany that permitted him to wage war? To answer this question, we must elaborate on our discussion in the first chapter on how Hitler came to power. I shall also add certain observations on the nature of Hitler's rule that so far could be only hinted at. Moreover, in discussing this question we shall find ourselves in the midst of a current controversy among historians.

Our second question concerns the external conditions of Hitler's waging the war. Our point of departure will be that it is inconceivable that one man acting arbitrarily should have been able to unleash the Second World War in all its theaters, in Europe, East Asia, and the other parts of the world. Apart from Hitler's will, there must have been preconditions that permitted him to act as he did. The usual next step from this point is a study of the attitudes of the other powers that facilitated or hindered Hitler's war plans, but I shall not take this much trodden path. I shall not enter into the diplomatic history of the interwar period. Instead I shall investigate why the war was fought in the last analysis and then assess Hitler's role in it.

Before taking up the first question we must briefly review Hitler's war plans, which he formulated in the 1920s. Without knowing his war plans we cannot evaluate how he prepared for, initiated, and conducted the war. Although it is important and, incidentally, fascinating to learn how he developed his plans, we shall consider only his final conception, which he reached between 1924 and 1928.

HITLER'S PLANS FOR WAR

Hitler's ultimate goal was the establishment of a greater Germany than had ever existed before in history. The way to this greater Germany was a war of conquest fought mainly at the expense of Soviet Russia. It was in the east of the European continent that the German nation was to gain living space (*Lebensraum*) for generations to come. This expansion would in turn provide the foundation for Germany's renewed position as a world power. Militarily the war would be easy because Germany would be opposed only by a disorganized country of Jewish Bolsheviks and incompetent Slavs. Politically, however, certain preconditions had to be met. The first was Germany's internal consolidation and rearmament. The second was a diplomatic situation in which Germany could not itself be attacked while it was attacking Soviet Russia.

The country most likely to oppose Germany's expansion in the east was France because that expansion would give Germany a dominant position in Europe that France could not tolerate. France, therefore, had to be eliminated as a military power in a preliminary campaign prior to the war proper. As Hitler saw it, this preliminary contest with France, although of subordinate interest only, would be a much bigger risk than the war against Russia—militarily because France was a great power, and politically because France had allies. France could, however, be isolated because there were frictions within the World War I alliance, with both Italy and Britain. The precondition for the defeat of France, which in turn was the precondition for the war against Russia, was therefore the conclusion of agreements with Italy and Britain.

These agreements would be based on the assumption that the three partners would expand in different directions: Germany toward the continental east, England overseas, and Italy in the Mediterranean and toward Africa. Thus they would not interfere with each other. Since their interests were compatible, so Hitler reasoned, Germany would be given a free hand on the Continent if it would renounce all claims on southern Tirol to Italy and avoid any rivalry with Britain overseas.

Hitler's program of foreign policy was thus divided into three major phases. During the first phase, Germany had to achieve internal consolidation and rearmament and to conclude agreements with Britain and Italy. During the second phase Germany had to defeat France in a preliminary engagement. Then the great war of conquest against Russia could take place during the third and final phase. Even a cursory glance at the diplomatic and military history of the Third Reich demonstrates that this program served as an outline of those German policies that were defined by Hitler himself, and there is ample documentary evidence to prove that he always kept this outline in mind. It was, of course, not a timetable or even a detailed prospectus, but a definite and structured list of objectives, priorities, and conditions.

How could Hitler have managed to implement his plan for German expansion? We shall try to answer this question by imagining the potential risks and impediments. Hitler's first problem was to remain in control of the state power. This condition is usually overlooked because as we look back we see Hitler firmly in control of the government until 1945, but Hitler's position was by no means certain in 1933, as he well knew. It is hardly an exaggeration to say that Hitler was always haunted by the fear of being overthrown. The men who had brought him to power were basically his rivals. They intended to use him to promote the conservative restoration they had striven for since 1930. But at the same time they hoped to do away with him as soon as they could. It is easy to say that they underestimated him. It is much less easy to explain how he remained in office and gradually seized more and more power.

What were the sources of his strength? Who supported him? There were, first of all, his followers in the Nazi party. But representing only a third of the nation, they had not been strong enough, as we have seen, to bring him to power. There were, then, his Conservative party allies, who had entered into a coalition government with him. But they did not want what he wanted. This was a peculiar and insecure basis of power. Usually a ruler is supported by a particular group or class united by a common interest. By contrast, Hitler was supported by two groups whose interests were not only different but conflicting. He thus ran the risk of disappointing one or the other or both of them and consequently of losing their support.

Hitler turned the weakness of this power base to his advantage, by catering to the conflicting interests of the two groups simultaneously, thus playing them against each other. It is true that he had no other viable choice. But whether he pursued this course intentionally or not, it provided him with a certain amount of independence from both. If the Nazi party had won a majority in parliament or in Germany, he would have been dependent on it to a considerable degree. But the fact that he was supported by his own followers on the one hand and by the conservatives on the other laid the first foundation of his independence. I shall illustrate this by a few examples.

He flattered the conservatives by opening the new Reichstag in an impressive ceremony held at the old Prussian residence in Potsdam, thus nourishing their hope that he would restore the monarchy. Simultaneously he promised his followers to provide them with work and bread, talked about a "national revolution," and let his storm troopers loose for the first anti-Jewish riot. At the same time he gave rearmament orders to industry, new assignments to the army, protection to civil servants—in sum, everything to everybody.

On May 1, 1933, he provided the working class with a national holiday celebrating labor, and the next day he dissolved the trade unions. In July he concluded a concordat with the Vatican, thus boosting his international respectability while also dissolving the last remnants of the Catholic Center Party. In September he granted a new basic law to the peasants. On June 30, 1934, he decimated the leadership of his party's army, the storm troopers; he thereby obliged the regular army to increased loyalty, but not without also reinforcing his own police, the SS, who persecuted his remaining domestic enemies.

These few examples should suffice to demonstrate that Hitler was not the representative of one class or one group alone—neither of industry nor of the middle class, neither of agriculture nor of the army. He served or menaced all of them, giving something here, taking something there, always careful not to side with any one of them completely. We repeat that he had no alternative. No group was strong enough to sustain him alone. They paralyzed each other, and that fact was his opportunity, which he skillfully exploited.

That possibility was the result of the peculiar situation I have characterized as the stalemate of the Weimar Republic. Neither of the two leading groups in Germany was strong enough to rule the state alone, but each was strong enough to prevent the other from doing so. It can be seen in history that such a situation is often the breeding ground of the ruler who is called a Bonapartist by Marx and Engels and whom I shall call a monocrat, a ruler who rules without the support of any one class alone but instead with the support of two or more classes with conflicting interests. I shall not enter into the details of the complicated theory of Bonapartism as it was developed by a number of sociologists in the nineteenth century.[2] I shall simply say that this theory has provided me with an explanation of Hitler's rule. He came to power in a stalemate. He was endowed with a certain charisma. He exploited his original basis of power by not relying on one group alone but instead serving several groups simultaneously, playing them against each other, and thus acquiring a certain independence that I call monocracy.

The term must not be understood to mean that a monocrat can do whatever he wants. He must take into account the wishes and interests of his supporters. But he is free from the need to reach an understanding with them on the political course he pursues. And so, after a certain time, he gains an enormous liberty of action. He remains in power as long as he is not overthrown, which is his permanent and only risk.

It is well known that there were no decision-making bodies in the Third Reich. I have mentioned this fact already as far as the party was concerned, and the same held for the government. This condition is one of the signs of a monocracy. After 1933 the cabinet met less and less frequently—it never discussed policy planning anyway—and finally held its last meeting in 1938. Hitler preferred to deal separately with his ministers, generals, party leaders, and other coworkers.

Another sign of monocracy related to the lack of decision-making bodies is a considerable degree of anarchy. Conflicting interests lead to conflicting authorities. The competencies are not clearly divided. The result is bureaucratic chaos, a constant struggle among offices and agencies. It is important to understand that this again is both in the nature of monocracy and in the interest of the monocrat.

This simple fact has been obscured by a recent controversy among historians.[3] The anarchic state of administration has always been noted by scholars and others and was even regretted and criticized by some Nazis. It has been defined by some historians as polycracy, a term that was already being used by a leading Nazi professor of constitutional law.[4] There can indeed be no doubt that the regime can justly be called polycratic. This is so far only a question of labels. But some historians have deduced from the term *polycracy* that decisions were made by conflicting authorities, that Hitler consequently did not and could not determine the course of policy, that he was driven into decisions instead of making them himself, and that in the last resort he could be defined as a weak dictator, as Hans Mommsen, a protagonist of the polycratic school, has put it.[5]

This school of thought entered into a heated and sometimes bitter debate with another school that maintained that Hitler had a definite program and carried it out by regularly making the appropriate decisions. The two antagonistic schools were designated by Tim Mason as the functionalists and the intentionalists, and it is indeed true that two fundamentally different interpretations of the Third Reich were developed by them—not least with regard to the decision concerning the Holocaust, which I shall discuss in the following chapter.

It is my opinion that the controversy is based on a profound misunderstanding on both sides. It would have been a misunderstanding if the so-called intentionalists had assumed that we can explain Hitler's acts by demonstrating that he had intentions. They would have neglected the fact that men can act only under certain conditions of support or compliance and that these conditions have to be demonstrated as well. On the other hand, it is a misunderstanding if the functionalists assume that in a polycratic regime the decisions are necessarily made in a polycratic way, that is, by conflicting authorities. There is abundant evidence that all the major decisions in the Third Reich were made by Hitler, and there is equally abundant evidence that the regime was largely anarchic and can thus be described as a polycracy. The misunderstanding is to suppose that the two observations are contradictory and that only one of them can be true.

According to my interpretation there is no contradiction between monocracy as I have defined it and polycracy. On the contrary, polycracy is the very condition of monocracy. The monocrat comes to power on a polycratic basis, supported by conflicting groups that paralyze each other, and he maintains his power by ruling polycratically—that is, by playing the conflicting groups against each other. It is precisely this method that permits him to make the major decisions alone. But even then he is, as I have said, not omnipotent. He has to take the wishes and interests of his supporters into account. A monocrat's rule is always risky. Let me now illustrate this interpretation by examining a few examples of how Hitler prepared and conducted the war according to his intentions.

GRADUAL DISCLOSURE OF OBJECTIVES

It can be said that Hitler's takeover came to an end in February 1938, when he finally gained complete control over the army and foreign affairs. He did so by means of the Fritsch crisis.[6] The crisis started when General von Blomberg, the minister of war, married a woman who did not suit the moral code of the army, which was not Hitler's code at all. He nevertheless exploited the situation by dismissing or accepting the resignation of the minister of war, Blomberg, the commander in chief of the army, Fritsch, who in an intrigue typical of a polycracy was accused of being a homosexual, and finally the foreign minister, Neurath, as well. All three belonged to the old conservative elites appointed by Hindenburg.

Hitler himself took command of the armed forces by abolishing the office of the minister of war altogether, and he placed a loyal follower of his, Ribbentrop, at the head of the Foreign Office. In the turmoil Göring also denounced Fritsch in order to succeed Blomberg, and Hitler again played the rivals against each other. He had thus considerably consolidated his power by exploiting a crisis within the traditional army and by exploiting a rivalry within the polycratic regime.

Significantly, it was then that Hitler held the last cabinet meeting and soon afterward declared his decision to wage war against Czechoslovakia, France's only reliable ally to the east. He was prevented from doing so, however. It was not only, and probably not even primarily, the determination of Chamberlain that much to Hitler's regret forced him to accept the Munich Agreement in September 1938. It was also, and probably decisively, internal opposition. General Beck, the chief of the general staff of the army, feared that a war against

Czechoslovakia might lead to another world war, which Germany would again lose; he protested and finally resigned.[7] Moreover, the German public appeared to be put off by the prospect of another war, particularly during a parade that Hitler observed in Berlin in September 1938. He had overrated his backing and had to give in.

It is not altogether false, therefore, to call him a weak dictator. As late as 1938 he had not been strong enough to change ministers at will, and he had also not been strong enough to wage war at will. But much of his strength lay precisely in his weakness. It enabled him to conceal his ultimate goals and disclose them only gradually. It also enabled him to order certain acts without being identified with them. Let us consider two examples. First, when the mentally ill were killed by the tens of thousands at the beginning of the war, the practice met with widespread opposition, but Hitler was generally not identified with it. As documentary evidence let us consider a letter written by one leading Nazi woman to another: "People are still clinging to the hope that the führer knows nothing about these things, that he cannot possibly know, otherwise he would stop them." The writer continues, "The matter must be brought to the attention of the führer before it is too late and there must be a way for the voice of the German people to reach the ear of its führer."[8]

This letter represents a double misconception. Hitler not only already knew what was supposed to be brought to his attention, but also had issued the orders for the offending policy. But he also heard the voice of the people and, most important, ordered the killing operation to be stopped. He then transferred the personnel and the equipment to the east and used them to kill the Jews. Once more he had turned a weakness to his advantage. Against the functionalist interpretation it should be stressed that internal opposition could at times prevent Hitler from doing certain things, but it could not force a course of action upon him.

The second example shows that not only the public but also his most intimate collaborators were often not aware of his aims. When after the fall of France in the summer of 1940 Hitler declared that he would now attack the Soviet Union, we might assume that no one close to Hitler was surprised. In fact, however, many including Ribbentrop were unpleasantly surprised and suggested that at least Britain should be defeated first. This advice had to be taken seriously, since Hitler had always asserted that Germany could not wage a war on two fronts. Thus his predicament was both interior and exterior. He had to convince his collaborators and also himself. He sensed the danger and yet found an ingenious solution. He presented the war against Russia as the best and indeed only means to defeat Britain.

Britain's hope, he argued to his generals on July 31, 1940, is Russia and America. If and when the Russian hope vanishes, the American hope will vanish as well, because the defeat of Russia will upgrade Japan in East Asia on a tremendous scale.[9] In other words, Hitler presented the war against Russia in conventional strategic terms and did not disclose his real aims, although he occasionally hinted at them. Only when he had convinced the army of the necessity and the feasibility of the Russian campaign and when the preparations were almost completed did he disclose in spring 1941 that this war would not be a conventional one. Contrary to his own earlier statements and probably also contrary to his own expectations, he now proclaimed that fierce resistance was to be expected. He thus succeeded in gaining for Himmler and the SS special powers to kill political commissars in the Red Army and Jewish Bolshevik officials.[10]

Once more it was only after the initial success of the campaign that he extended his killing orders and in a meeting with his top aides on July 16, 1941, finally disclosed his real aims in Russia.[11] It must be clear to us, he said, that we will never relinquish these territories. We must transform the newly won eastern territories into a garden of Eden; they are vital to us, whereas overseas colonies play an altogether subordinate role. And then he appointed his own commissars to rule over the conquered lands. This was the living space (*Lebensraum*), the arable soil for the German peasant he had demanded in so many words in the second volume of *Mein Kampf* in 1925 and in many subsequent speeches until 1930.

It is extremely doubtful whether even his most intimate collaborators after he came to power were always mindful of what he had demanded before. Certainly he had sometimes made allusions to his eastern goal. When he met with military leaders for the first time on February 3, 1933, he declared it his aim to regain political power for Germany. He then more or less casually asked how that power should be used once it was won. He discussed several options, replied that the issue could not yet be decided, and suddenly added, "Perhaps for conquest of new living space in the East and its ruthless Germanization." The generals did not take him seriously, however, and even made jokes about him.[12]

It cannot be ruled out that he had initiated some of his closest collaborators in the party such as Hess, Göring, Himmler, or Goebbels to his plans. It sometimes appears that they had been admitted to their führer's secrets, but there is no direct documentary evidence of such special briefings. It is more likely that they too were informed only gradually and as circumstances required. It might be expected that they had understood what he had in mind by reading his book. But even of this there is hardly any evidence.

The history of *Mein Kampf* becomes significant at this point. It went through many editions basically unaltered, was distributed in millions of copies, and yet was generally not read or at all odds not taken seriously and, what is more important, not discussed in public. Only banalities were quoted from it and used as slogans. It would have been un-

thinkable, for example, for a convinced and loyal Nazi jour-
nalist to write after the beginning of the Russian campaign,
quoting chapter and verse, that the führer was now carrying
out what he had announced in his book with such admirable
clarity. Such an article, although exactly in line with the book,
would not have been welcome, for the war was presented as a
preemptive war against an imminent Soviet attack. There are
no indications that the event was interpreted in light of the
book even by inner circles of the Third Reich or in private
conversations, correspondence, and the like. Only a few foreign observers drew the obvious lessons, the outstanding
example being a tiny Oxford pamphlet on world affairs published by R. C. K. Ensor in July 1939 and entitled "Herr
Hitler's Self-Disclosure in *Mein Kampf.*" It is safe to say that
in Germany no one drew a line from Hitler's book to his acts.
Certainly, there is no evidence of it.

Hitler only gradually disclosed his objectives in waging this
war. He first presented his aim as the peaceful revision of the
Versailles treaty. He then proclaimed it his purpose to unite all
Germans in one state, basing his policy on the right of self-
determination. This right was contested by Britain and France
when he undertook to liberate the Germans in Poland. Thus
war broke out, and France was defeated in June 1940. Since
Britain still resisted his peace initiatives and could not be
invaded, he started the war against Russia. His reason was
officially to preempt an imminent attack by Russia. Among
his top collaborators his reason was understood to be to
discourage Britain before the United States was ready to enter
the war and to enable Germany to become economically
self-sufficient so that it could continue the war indefinitely.
This autarkic land base acquired officially in self-defense could
then finally be proclaimed as the future living space for the
German nation. With the exception of the war against Russia
being presented as a means to discourage Britain, this neces-

sary self-defense was the official version of Hitler's war and there is no doubt that it was accepted by the majority of the Germans.

Hitler was occasionally more explicit in secret speeches to his inner circle. The documentary evidence of this may not be complete, but it is large enough to show that his aims had not changed since the 1920s. Even so, he remained vague about his ultimate goals, argued circumstantially on most points, and never again unveiled the broad conception as he had in his book. Even in the conference best known in this respect, that of November 5, 1937, with his top diplomatic and military collaborators, he devoted only a few minutes to the acquisition of living space and did not mention Russia, but discussed at length several options regarding France and France's allies.[13] His remarks on this occasion could also be understood as an admonition to accelerate the process of rearmament.

Generally speaking, Hitler found the necessary support because he had won authority over the German people. In *Mein Kampf* he had reflected on building authority. Its first foundation, he said, was popularity, its second was force, and its third was tradition.[14] He clearly lacked tradition, although he tried to claim it at times by posing as the successor of Frederick the Great or Bismarck. He acquired popularity and force, the latter mainly in the form of terror, and exploited them both fully. As far as the people were concerned, his rule was indeed based on a combination of popularity and terror.

But the assent and obedience of the people at large were not enough. He also needed the support of the party and that of the state apparatus represented by the army, the civil service, and the economy. The party was his smallest problem. He was its uncontested leader by 1933, and after the liquidation of Röhm in 1934 there was never the least attempt to resist him. The party leaders may have been fighting each other with extreme bitterness, thus presenting a fine object lesson in polycracy, but their loyalty toward the führer was never in doubt.

The army was Hitler's most difficult partner, belonging as it did entirely to the conservative segment of German society. Because the military had been humiliated by the defeat of 1918 and reduced under the Weimar Republic, they generally welcomed Hitler when he promised them new glamour. They were then worried by his rival army, the militialike SA, and relieved when he abolished it in 1934. They were worried again when immediately afterward he started to establish another competing armed force, the SS-Verfügungstruppe, which was indeed meant to be an emergency force against internal disorder or attempts to overthrow the regime.[15] The army insisted on being the only armed force and much of the early opposition to Hitler among the military, particularly by Beck, resulted from this competition.

The generals later resisted Hitler's war plans in 1938 and contributed to his abandoning them. They resisted his plans again in the fall of 1939 when he wanted the army to attack France immediately after the Polish campaign. He postponed the attack and then made of it his most brilliant victory. That victory raised him to the summit of his prestige, the more since he personally had devised the successful operational plan. Many officers who were later to oppose him again confessed on this earlier occasion that they had been fainthearted and unjust to the führer, and he consequently had no serious difficulty in leading them into Russia.

The opposition revived when he visibly started losing the war. It culminated in the attempt on his life on July 20, 1944. The July plot against him has largely been appraised in moral terms since the war. There is no denying its moral aspects. It must be recognized, however, that the main thrust of the conspiracy was not against the criminality of the regime in 1944 any more than in 1938. It was, rather, a desperate attempt by the conservative circles that had brought Hitler to power to regain a minimum of control over such vital questions as whether Germany should start a war or should end it when it was lost.

To sum up, the relationship between Hitler and the army was not easy, its support never a matter of course. He won its support from one juncture to the next only by flattering and obliging its leaders and not least by corrupting them. He corrupted them personally by cash awards and grand decorations, but above all and principally by making them his accomplices. This happened for the first time during the liquidation of Röhm, in which the army took an active part. But it soon became a favorite technique that he used on many other occasions. Hitler did not like to rely on friends who shared his views, and, indeed, he had almost no friends. Instead he relied on accomplices whom he had so corrupted that they could no longer desert him. He liked people to burn their bridges behind them. That was the kind of loyalty he understood. At times he even said so. For example, he always disliked the idea of collaboration with the French. But when Himmler began to collaborate with the French police in 1942, Hitler applauded him, saying, "The police are more hated than anything else in the country. They seek support from an authority stonger than their own state: from us. They will one day implore us not to leave the country."[16]

It is quite possible that in Hitler's view the extermination of the Jews also had the advantage of corrupting his collaborators, forcing them to stay with him until the end. Both Goebbels and Himmler sensed this and expressed themselves accordingly. This attitude was certainly part of Hitler's personal character, but it should not be overlooked that it also resulted from the nature of his rule. He had no supporters he could rely on completely, only occasional to be exploited and, from time to time, corrupted.

In the case of the civil service and the business sector, Hitler won their support largely by leaving them alone. They certainly were important to him as instruments, but he had neither the intention to reform them nor the need to use them for extraordinary operations. The administration has been aptly described by Ernst Fraenkel as the normal part of Hitler's dual state, the other part being his special outfits such as the SS.[17] Business was not subjected to expropriations or similar measures and was permitted to profit. Admittedly these remarks are superficial; yet they may suffice for our purposes, since these two sectors presented no serious obstacles to Hitler when he prepared for and waged his war.

The picture presented so far of an almost innocent people and a reluctant army being drawn into a war by a sly and ruthless monocrat is likely to raise the liveliest objections, particularly as it does not take into account the problem of shared moral responsibility or guilt. It is indeed my conviction that it is not the historian's business to pass value judgments or moral verdicts. As an individual he may do so, just as everyone does. As a scholar he has to explain how things past could have happened, and in so doing he may safely rely on the general assumption that the Germans living under Hitler were not better or worse than those who lived before or after them or other people in their times, but that they lived under special conditions. It is these conditions that the historian must make comprehensible.

THE CLIMATE OF WAR IN THE WORLD

I have so far analyzed or tried to analyze the conditions that enabled Hitler to come to power and to wage war. But I may have concentrated too much on him. I have not raised the question whether there was something deeper in German history or German society that drove it into the Second World War and caused it to choose Hitler as its appropriate instrument. More specifically, I stated in the first chapter that one condition of Hitler's coming to power was the founding of the

Nazi party, and that the Nazi party as well as Hitler's political career obviously resulted from Germany's defeat and intended revenge. We then saw that the Nazi movement alone
was not strong enough to bring Hitler to power. But it remains
to inquire whether there was a tacit understanding between
those who voted for Hitler and the remaining two thirds of
the population on a war of revenge—in other words, whether
those who did not vote for Hitler may have voted for another
government that certainly would have been different from Hitler's but would also have led the country into war.

These are serious but hypothetical questions, and I can see
no way of answering them verifiably. What the fact-bound
researcher can state and perhaps explain is only that the governments of the Weimar Republic did not seriously prepare
for a war, whereas Hitler did. Nevertheless, an indirect approach to this problem may be possible. An analysis of the
external conditions of Hitler's acts may enable us to answer
by analogy the question about the more profound origins of
the war.

Usually the question of the external conditions of Hitler's
war is taken to mean why the world was not able to prevent
him from unleashing that war which he so openly described
in the 1920s and prepared for in the 1930s. The popular
answer is still the one expressed in the theme of the first
volume of Winston Churchill's memoirs: "How the English-
speaking peoples through their unwisdom, carelessness and
good nature allowed the wicked to rearm."[18] Like Churchill,
others have developed this theme by vituperating against the
policies of appeasement, the lack of resolution, and the like.
The scholarly answer along these lines is provided by studies
of the diplomatic, social, and economic history of the interwar
period, stressing the demographic weakness of France, the
economic postwar crises in Britain, American isolationism,
and the like. Without denying the importance of any of these
factors, which in varying degrees did contribute to the war, I

propose to consider an even more fundamental condition of the war. This consideration should prompt us to reflect on Hitler's role anew and to see it in a different light.

If we say that Hitler's war was a war of conquest or of territorial expansion, we must not overlook that two other countries fought similar wars at the same time and even started them before Hitler started his. Japan expanded into Manchuria in 1931 and opened hostilities against China in 1937. Mussolini launched his war of conquest against Ethiopia in 1935. In each case the aim was territorial expansion. Although Hitler favored these expansionist efforts and later concluded alliances with these states, it clearly cannot be said that he provoked these wars. Neither can it be said that these wars provoked his, which he had envisaged so much earlier. But there seems to be a similarity among them.

It may be said that the Second World War was characterized on one side by the regional hegemonic ambitions of Japan, Germany, and Italy, all three of which attempted to achieve a new predominance in areas adjoining their own national territory: Japan in the so-called Greater East Asia Coprosperity Sphere (Daitōa kyōeiken), Germany in a Greater German or Germanic Empire (Grossdeutsches or Grossgermanisches Reich), and Italy in a new Roman Empire (Impero). These three expansionist states stood opposed to three other states that obviously were not out to expand territorially, namely, Britain, France, and the United States. They later expressed this clearly in their joint program. In the Atlantic Charter of August 14, 1941, the heads of government of Britain and the United States (at the time France had left the war) declared as their first point: "Their countries seek no aggrandizement, territorial or other." And indeed although these countries emerged from the war victorious, they did not exploit their victory for any territorial expansion worth mentioning.

This cannot be said of the Soviet Union. Unlike the three

states defined as expansionist, the USSR did not enter the war for the sake of territorial expansion but simply because it was attacked. Unlike its Western allies, however, it made ambitious use of the war for purposes of territorial expansion. By 1939 and 1940, protected by its treaty with Germany, it had embarked on an expansionist policy. Its territorial gains at the moment of victory were important and they can be described in detail. In 1945 Russia won back more or less all the territories it had lost in the course of the twentieth century, namely, those that had been lost in Asia after the defeat by Japan in 1905 and those lost in Europe after the revolution of 1917. Its expansionism may therefore be called revisionist, whereas the three aggressors had fought for new conquests. Thus we are confronted with a three-part division of the Great Powers involved in World War II. The three Great Powers that desired to change the territorial status quo in their own favor stood opposed by three others that desired to preserve the status quo, and between the two stood the Soviet Union with a special attitude, which was also expressed in its shift of alliance in 1941.

If we want to explain this we may well find relevant similarities in the histories of the seven Great Powers. Germany, Italy, and Japan had entered upon the stage of world politics at almost the same time around 1870—Germany and Italy by their national unification, Japan by its opening to foreign contacts and the ensuing Meiji Restoration. At that time the other four Great Powers had long since been in existence with a long period of territorial expansion behind them, Russia and the United States having penetrated their respective continents, and England and France having engaged in colonial imperialism.

In that age after 1870, all the Great Powers may be called expansionist. There was a new rush for colonies everywhere. After the First World War, however, the Western powers changed their attitude. They established the League of Nations, which by its very nature was an instrument for the maintenance of the status quo. But the three later aggressors challenged it after some years. All of them were disappointed by the outcome of the war, although Italy and Japan had been among the victors. All three experienced economic crises, social unrest, political instability, and the establishment of authoritarian regimes. All three left the League of Nations under protest—Japan and Germany in 1933, Italy in 1937—and launched a new expansionism. The rest of the story is too well known to need retelling here.

To conclude this chapter we must now return to its beginning, to Hitler. We have seen how Hitler drew Germany into war; he had a plan and carried it out. But we have also seen that there was a longstanding tendency toward expansion not only in Germany but also in two other countries constituted at about the same time, a tendency that led them into similar wars of conquest meant to establish similar empires. We cannot overlook or minimize the three-way differences—Italy's weakness, Japan's special problems, and Germany's exceptional aggressiveness and brutality. And yet we are bound to be intrigued and irritated by the fundamental analogy. How are we to assess Hitler's role within this global perspective?

He undoubtedly developed a program of his own, individually and alone. But his program must have coincided with the deeper tendencies and ambitions of his country and of his time. We may not be able to explain this, and yet we have to recognize it. Was he an author or an executor, a producer or a product? Was he so successful for a long time as an author because he was executing deeper tendencies? Or had he simply a better understanding than most of his contemporaries of the requirements and the possibilities of his time?

These are fundamental questions about not only the role of the individual in history but also historical understanding in general. We may well reach their limits here, and I for my part and for the time being shall end with these questions.

3
Hitler Orders the Holocaust

The extermination of the European Jews in the Second
World War, or more precisely the German attempt to kill as
many of them as possible, an undertaking unique in human
history that has come to be called not very appropriately the
Holocaust, has in recent years become the subject of specific
historical research. For a long time it was neither grasped
fully in its tremendous importance nor subjected to close and
detailed scrutiny. The historians, to be sure only a few of
them, limited themselves to establishing the bare facts, which
are now more or less well known, while the general public if
interested at all looked in a sort of arresting horror at the
event as something metahistorical and discussed the moral
aspects of it alone.[1] This is now changing. We begin to ask
more specific questions. One of them is how the decisions to
carry out the extermination were made. It is just this intri-
guing question, which has recently become the subject of a
controversy—actually the first scholarly controversy in the
matter—that I shall deal with here.

Perhaps for no other problem of such magnitude in modern

history is the documentation so poor. There are various reasons for this. The operation was ultrasecret. Consequently as little as possible was written down. Much was transacted orally, particularly on the highest level. Of the few relevant documents, many were destroyed before the war ended. And of those that survive, many contain code names and terms that further hamper the task of clearly establishing their contents. Moreover, many of the persons directly involved died before they could be interrogated. Of those who survived, most answered evasively. But even those who were ready to talk were often not questioned precisely enough, for their interrogators were not interested in the kinds of details that historians would want to clarify. Many were then executed, and their knowledge disappeared with them.

Christopher Browning has aptly compared the historian of the Holocaust to the man in Plato's cave who sees only reflections and shadows, not the reality behind them.[2] He must reconstruct the reality by extrapolation from events, documents, and testimony originating outside the inner circle where the killing orders were issued. Peripheral events, documents, and testimony: such are indeed, and in order of importance, the sources of our knowledge about the unleashing of the Holocaust. To proceed on this basis requires an extraordinary degree of circumspection and precision. If we want to know how the decisions behind the Holocaust were made, we must not only ask when they were made. We must frame our questions carefully. Because the undertaking was unprecedented, we must presume that the decisions were taken in an unprecedented way. We must, in other words, not anticipate any normal procedure of decision making that we know from experience in other fields.

The first question is the most fundamental: Did Hitler order the Holocaust? I shall not trouble to refute the indefensible allegation of some that Hitler did not know what happened. But did he order it? This has been denied by Martin Broszat and other so-called functionalists, whose views I discussed in the preceding chapter.[3] Broszat's interpretation is that the killing program evolved gradually from a series of separate killing operations in 1941 and 1942 and from the impossibility of further evacuation and resettlement of Jews in Europe. This is a serious proposition based on a lot of documentary evidence, or perhaps even more on the gaps in the historical record. Although I shall not accept this functionalist interpretation, I admit that it has certainly refined our question. We must ask not simply whether Hitler ordered the Holocaust but whether the Holocaust was improvised or premeditated. The clarification should prove illuminating but will have to be subjected to further scrutiny, since the improvisation may have been premeditated.

Once the general question is answered, specific questions will have to be put. It can be ruled out that a single killing order was given. The extermination was divided into several phases and covered a wide variety of methods and victims. We must therefore assume a correspondingly wide variety of orders extending over a period of several months. We must ask what those orders were, to whom they were given, and how they were transmitted to those who carried them out.

To begin with, I shall briefly summarize Hitler's views on what he called the Jewish question.[4] This is relevant for at least three reasons. First, he was the head of the state and the government and wielded dictatorial power in Germany at that time. Second, he was the only Nazi and as far as I know the only anti-Semite who had ever expressly advocated systematic killing by the state as a means of resolving the Jewish question. And third, what he called the *Entfernung,* or removal of the Jews, was of supreme importance to him. He had set himself two goals, a war of conquest and the elimination of the Jews, and regarded all other aspects of politics simply as means to achieve these goals.

The first relevant document, indeed the first record of his

political activity, is a letter dated September 16, 1919, in which he wrote that the ultimate goal of anti-Semitism must unalterably be the elimination of the Jews altogether.[5] The context as well as his anti-Jewish pronouncements of the following years demonstrate with sufficient clarity what he primarily meant: The Jews living in Germany were to be removed from Germany to other countries.

After 1924 the term *elimination* sometimes took on the meaning of killing, although certain formulations of his suggest that he had had this solution in mind even before 1924. In the second volume of *Mein Kampf* he wrote that the elimination could only be achieved "by the sword" and called the needful procedure "bloody."[6] He now also elaborated at length on his belief that the Jewish question had an importance for the whole world, and he complained that the opportunity had not been taken to kill about twelve thousand Jews by poison gas at the beginning of and during World War I.[7] If this is taken literally, he meant that killing a part of the Jewish community in Germany during the First World War (twelve thousand out of a total that he estimated at six hundred thousand) would have been a means to win that war.[8] There was also a vague suggestion that it was desirable that other nations eliminate their Jews as well.

In his books, particularly the one written in 1928 but not published until 1961, Hitler explained in detail why he wanted the Jews to be eliminated.[9] It must not be overlooked that his hatred was certainly irrational but specific as well. In his view, the Jews were a people or race, not a religious community. Being a people, they participated in the general struggle among peoples for power. But having no territorial state, they could not participate in the normal form of that struggle, which was the struggle for territorial living space. Thus they fought for power by other means. The adversary in their struggle was not this or that nation but all nations—the principle of nation as such, the law of nature and history. Hence the

Jews were not an enemy of the German nation alone but of all mankind, and their elimination was not only a national but a universal task.

If we pursue this reasoning a bit further we may say that the elimination of the German Jews was in the interest of Germany, since they undermined Germany's capacity to struggle for living space. Consequently, their transfer into countries that were Germany's actual or potential opponents in the struggle for living space meant a weakening of these countries and was thus an advantage to Germany. But Hitler did not say so explicitly. He wished other countries to eliminate their Jews as well. This is the basic contradiction of Hitler's anti-Semitism. As a German he wanted the elimination of the German Jews before all others. But as far as the Jews were concerned, he felt that he could not afford to be a German alone. The Jewish question was so important to him that he sought the elimination of all Jews. In July 1941 he declared to a foreign statesman that he would confront each state with the demand to eliminate its Jews.[10] In October of the same decisive year he said that he was doing humanity a service by exterminating this pest.[11]

Rudolph Binion has convincingly demonstrated that Hitler did not succeed in solving this contradiction.[12] Thus in principle and from the outset his racial policy was less clear than his foreign policy. As for the war of conquest, he was to pursue the interests of Germany exclusively; hence his task was easy. As for the Jews, he had to pursue the interests of both Germany and humanity at once; hence this task was difficult. At times he set his priorities, at times he did not, and this confusion marked his acts.

Immediately after he came to power his task was easy. He had to remove the German Jews from political standing and if possible from Germany. His policy pursued these goals. By 1938 approximately 150,000 Jews or almost one third of the country's total Jewish population had left Germany. But with the annexation of Austria another 200,000 were added. Although a quarter of them left the country within six months, by the end of 1938 Greater Germany had once again as many Jews as Germany had had in 1933. The task seemed unending.

For whatever reasons, after the annexation of Austria and especially after the Munich Conference of September 29, 1938, the anti-Jewish policy became more intense. By March of that year Hitler spoke with increased furor.[13] In June the Nazi leader and writer Rosenberg proposed Madagascar as a country of emigration.[14] In October Göring wanted the Jews to get out of the economy and if necessary to establish ghettos.[15] Then approximately seventeen thousand Jews holding Polish passports were deported from Germany to Poland.[16] This was a prelude to the November pogrom. A few days later Göring said that if war came, there would be a great settling of accounts with the Jews.[17] On November 24 Hitler told a foreign statesman that the Jewish question was a European problem.[18] On the same day the SS newspaper demanded total destruction of the German Jews if war came.[19] On January 21, 1939, Hitler told the Czech foreign minister that the Jews in Germany were going to be destroyed.[20] On January 24 Göring ordered Heydrich and Frick to prepare a solution of the Jewish question by emigration or evacuation.[21] Finally on January 30 Hitler publicly declared—or, as he put it, prophesied—that the result of another world war would be the destruction of the Jewish race in Europe.[22] What sounds so ominous in three of these proclamations is the projected relation between a war and the solution to the Jewish question. Hitler had drawn this connection in *Mein Kampf* and had redrawn it since on several occasions. On February 10, 1939, he repeated to commanding officers that the next struggle was going to be a racial war.[23]

When World War II broke out, there was no immediate action against the Jews. Despite Hitler's demand in 1926 for the destruction of the Jews, there was no pogrom and no Jews were killed. Instead, the government began killing mental patients by means of gas and deporting Jews. The main destination was occupied Poland, where the Nazis finally seemed to have found a convenient dumping ground for the Jews, whose numbers had once more increased after the recent territorial acquisitions. On September 21, 1939, Heydrich informed his subordinates that Hitler had permitted the deportation of the German Jews and of those Jews living in the annexed parts of Poland, apparently to the region near Cracow.[24] One week later the Soviets ceded the province of Lublin, and Hitler told Rosenberg the next day that he wished to remove all of German-controlled Jewry into this area between the Vistula and the Bug rivers.[25] On October 7 Himmler was appointed "Reich Commissar for the strengthening of German folkdom" and was charged with the task.[26]

The operation ran into countless difficulties, however, and turned out to be a failure. Hans Frank, the governor general of occupied Poland, which had been renamed the General Government, constantly complained that he could not settle those who had been or were to be deported.[27] To be sure, about 50 percent of the Jews and 10 percent of the Poles in the annexed Polish territories were deported and their homes given to German resettlers, who poured in at the same time from Russia and southeast Europe after an agreement concluded with the Soviet Union. But only a few thousand Jews from Austria, Moravia, and Pomerania could be deported. In March 1940 Göring stopped all deportations.[28] And Hitler told a Swedish visitor that a Jewish state around Lublin would never be a solution to the Jewish problem.[29]

After the fall of France, new prospects opened for disposing of Europe's Jews. Already on May 25, just a fortnight after the beginning of Germany's western campaign, Himmler delivered to Hitler a lengthy memorandum envisaging the emigration of all Jews to Africa or a colony.[30] On June 24, right after the armistice, Heydrich wrote to Ribbentrop that the problem—3¼ million Jews under German rule—could no longer be solved by emigration and therefore a territorial final solution became necessary.[31] Perhaps he wanted to induce the foreign minister to acquire such a territory from France during the expected peace talks.[32] The Madagascar plan was revived. It seems that Hitler had mentioned it to Mussolini on June 18.[33] He certainly mentioned it when he told Frank on July 8 that there would be no more transports of Jews into the General Government.[34]

German policy still appeared to be to get rid of the Jews by emigration or deportation. In July Jews from Alsace-Lorraine were deported into France proper, followed by those from southwest Germany in October.[35] But Vichy France was a limited dumping ground. And since the conclusion of a peace treaty turned out to be impossible, the Madagascar plan fell through. There is no indication that Hitler had ever intended it seriously.

The decisive change of policy came with the approach of the war against Russia. Military preparations for the campaign began in August 1940. In September Frank noted in his official diary that Hitler had devoted his special attention to the General Government, that the transport system there should be brought up to the standard of that of the Reich by June 1941, that a huge army comprising many divisions would be stationed there, that resettlements would cease and a plan to deport more than 350,000 Jews from Germany had been given up.[36] Evidently occupied Poland was becoming the base from which German troops would invade Russia. Understandably further resettlements were incompatible with this military assignment.

In November, however, Frank was told that he had to take in new settlers.[37] Hitler decided that sixty thousand Jews from Vienna were to be deported to the General Government.[38] But slightly over five thousand of them were in fact deported in February and March 1941.[39] Then the deportations were interrupted again, and Hitler told Frank on March 16 that an event was approaching that would mark a great change (he was referring, of course, to the beginning of the Russian campaign), and that the General Government would be the first region to be made free of Jews *(judenfrei)*.[40]

Three days before, Himmler had been given special responsibilities in the Russian campaign for which the *Einsatzgruppen* were established.[41] As will be seen, there is still controversy over what their orders were and when those orders were given. But it can safely be stated that one of their objectives was to kill Russian Jews. This again was inconsistent. Whereas Hitler had formerly depicted the Jews as a disintegrating factor in Russia, he now presented them as the backbone of Russian resistance, which had to be broken in order to defeat Russia. It would have been more consistent of him to let them escape so that they could continue their work of disintegration. Moreover, it was to be expected that the killings would not remain secret and thus would stiffen Russian resistance, as indeed they did.

The beginning of the Russian campaign marked a turning point in Germany's Jewish policy. Obviously a prior order had been given to kill Russian Jews. But the decisions concerning the Jews in the rest of Europe remain obscure.

On May 20, 1941, Heydrich's office sent out a strange circular letter according to which the emigration of Jews from France and Belgium was to be halted.[42] That was sensational enough, since emigration had always been promoted before then. But the reasons given in this strange letter were even stranger. It was said that according to information from Göring *(gemäss einer Mitteilung des Reichsmarschalls)*, the emigration of Jews from Germany was to be increased; emigration from France and Belgium was, therefore, to be prevented because it diminished the chances for German Jews to emigrate. It may be noted incidentally that the emigration of German Jews was not forbidden until October 1, 1941.[43] But then the letter from Heydrich's office gave a second, ominous reason for halting Jewish emigration from France and Belgium. It continued, "and in view of the undoubtedly imminent final solution of the Jewish question" (*und im Hinblick auf die zweifellos kommende Endlösung der Judenfrage*).

This is puzzling indeed. If that so-called final solution meant killing as many Jews as possible, then it was highly inconsistent to increase Jewish emigration from Germany. But perhaps the fact that Göring was mentioned as having referred to increased emigration offers a clue to an interpretation of the letter. We may tentatively hypothesize that both Göring and Heydrich had heard of Hitler's desire to proceed to the final solution now, and that Heydrich wanted to fulfill that desire while Göring wanted to obstruct it. Shortly before, Göring had been quoted as saying, "It is more important for us to win the war than to implement racial policy."[44] Certainly the competing offices of the Third Reich were also struggling against each other over the Jewish question and the priorities to be set. And another hypothesis may be derived from this letter, namely, that Hitler had not issued a formal order but had, in May 1941, expressed the desire to proceed to the final solution in the foreseeable future.

According to Frank, Hitler declared outright on June 19, three days before the Russian campaign began, that the Jews would be removed (*entfernt*) from the General Government in the foreseeable future and that the General Government should become a transit camp only (*nur noch gewissermassen Durchgangslager*).[45] This statement can be interpreted as a cynical metaphor for transit to death, and indeed the killing centers were sometimes called transit camps.[46] It can also be taken literally. On July 21 Hitler dropped a hint that the Jews could be sent to Siberia.[47] It cannot be ruled out that he thought of a defeated Soviet Union, east of the prospective German line from Arkhangelsk to Astrakhan, as yet another and final dumping ground for the Jews, where Stalin would have to accept them. It must not be forgotten that in July he expected the war in the east to be over within a few months; he would by then be far from having solved the Jewish question by mass killings, if they could be undertaken in wartime only.

In any case he was fully engaged in extermination by July 1941, but the sequence of orders remains obscure. Alfred Streim has argued recently in a detailed study that the *Einsatzgruppen* commanders were ordered by Heydrich in Berlin on June 17 to execute all Communist commissars and Jewish party and state officials and to provoke anti-Jewish pogroms, that this order was repeated by Heydrich on July 2, and that an order by Hitler, a *Führerbefehl*, to kill all Russian Jews including women and children was not given until some time between the end of July and the end of August 1941.[48] This corresponds largely, but not entirely, to the actual sequence of events.

On July 20 and 21, 1941, Himmler was in Lublin and may have instructed Odilo Globocnik, the higher SS and police leader there, to prepare for the extermination of the Polish Jews.[49] The extermination of Polish Jews began, however, at Chelmno in the annexed western Polish territories on December 8, whereas Globocnik's Operation Reinhard did not begin until February or March 1942. On July 22 Frank discussed preparations for the removal of the Jews from the General Government beginning with the Warsaw Ghetto.[50] But this evacuation, to Treblinka, did not actually begin until exactly a year later, on July 22, 1942.[51]

On July 31, 1941, Heydrich went to see Göring and had him sign an authorization fully prepared in advance to make all the necessary preparations for a total solution of the Jewish question in the area of Europe under German control.[52] Göring's signature probably enabled Heydrich to initiate the deportation of the German Jews. On August 18 Hitler promised Goebbels that the Jews of Berlin would be deported to the east immediately after the end of the eastern campaign.[53] Even so, the deportations began from Germany outside Berlin on October 15 and from Berlin on October 18. The first convoys went to Lódź, Minsk, and Riga. The first German Jews were shot near Kovno on November 25.

Both Rudolf Höss, the commander of Auschwitz, and Eichmann testified after the war that they were told by Himmler in the summer of 1941 that Hitler had ordered the final solution of the Jewish question. Höss was not pressed to be more specific. Eichmann specified that it had been about two or three months after the war against the Soviet Union had begun and that Hitler had ordered the physical liquidation of the Jews without, however, specifying which Jews were to be liquidated first.[54]

Thereafter the operation was no longer kept entirely secret. On November 16, 1941, Goebbels wrote in a lead article in his weekly newspaper *Das Reich* that Hitler's prophecy on January 30, 1939, of the destruction of the Jewish race in Europe was now coming true.[55] Two days later Rosenberg confidentially told a press conference of the biological extermination of European Jewry as a whole.[56] On December 14 Hitler agreed with Rosenberg that it was not appropriate to speak of extermination in public.[57]

On November 29 Heydrich sent out invitations to the Wannsee Conference scheduled to take place on December 9.[58] It was postponed later to January 20, 1942. The invitations were accompanied by copies of Göring's authorization of July 31, 1941. The importance of the Wannsee Conference should not be overrated. No decisions were made at the conference; its purpose was the briefing of officials and coordination of government agencies. One of its objectives may have been the inclusion of West European Jews in the final solution. On March 27 the first convoy of French Jews left Drancy, France, for Auschwitz, where mass killings had begun in February 1942.

In four public speeches during 1942 Hitler reminded his
listeners of his so-called prophecy of destruction of the Jews
of Europe. Unlike Goebbels, who always dated it correctly
from January 30, 1939, Hitler invariably misdated it to September 1 of that year. On that day, when the war against
Poland began, he had also spoken in the Reichstag but he had
not mentioned the Jewish question at all. There can be no
doubt that the misdating, which was repeated in the printed
versions of the speeches, was deliberate. Evidently he wanted
the extermination of the Jews to be seen in connection with
the beginning of the war.

We need not enter into the later stages of the Holocaust in
order to answer our questions. Apparently not just one order
was given to initiate it. And apparently its beginnings involved
considerable inconsistency, improvisation, and confusion.

This has led some of the so-called functionalist historians
to infer that the whole operation may not have been ordered
or premeditated at all. In order to avoid misunderstandings
it should be stressed that Martin Broszat, who has developed
this thesis most explicitly, does not deny Hitler's responsibility for or approval of the killings. Broszat's thesis is only that
they were proposed and initiated by others as well, that they
were not planned long in advance and initiated by a single
secret order.

There is some evidence for such an interpretation. On July
16, 1941, a relatively early date, officials close to the *Reichs-
statthalter* in Posen, in the annexed Polish territories, asked
Eichmann to consider seriously whether instead of letting the
Jews starve, it would not be more human to dispose of those
who could not work by a rapidly effective means.[59] Is it not
logical to infer—that is the functionalists' question—that the
final solution evolved gradually out of such proposals and the
resulting individual killing operations?

My first answer is that there is no evidence that there were
many such proposals or individual killing actions, and cer-

tainly not prior to the spring of 1941. Until that date, with the exception of the killings during the invasion of Poland in 1939, all officials in charge of the Jewish question, from Göring and Himmler to Heydrich and Eichmann, were fully involved in emigration, evacuation, or deportation, and there is no evidence that any one of them proposed or envisaged a different procedure. On the other hand, there is a great deal of evidence that at least some of them were shocked or even appalled when the final solution went into effect. To be sure, they did not disagree with it. But they agreed only reluctantly, referring time and again to an order given by Hitler. This is a strong indication that the idea did not originate with them.

In his secret speeches in 1943 and 1944 Himmler lamented many times that this order had been a burden for him, the hardest challenge of his life, or even the most dreadful task, the most dreadful order that could be assigned to an organization.[60] When Goebbels learned of Globocnik's action in the death camp of Belzec near Lublin, where mass killings in gas chambers had begun shortly after March 16, 1942, Goebbels wrote in his diary on March 27 that the procedure was barbarous, that Hitler's prophecy was coming true in the most dreadful manner, and that "the führer is the unrelenting protagonist and advocate of a radical solution."[61] Rosenberg, apparently after having been briefed by Hitler on the same question, noted in his diary on April 2, 1941, the stunted sentence: "What I do not want to write down today but will never forget."[62]

Before producing further evidence that Hitler was the prime and only instigator of the Holocaust, I shall briefly return to the killings in Poland in 1939. Again there is no evidence that they were proposed or initiated locally or by subordinate agencies. On the contrary, in a note of July 2, 1940, Heydrich described them as a political operation carried out by Himmler according to instructions (*Weisungen*) from Hitler, and he mentioned the term order (*Befehl*) twice.[63]

To sum up, my conclusion that the final solution was ordered by Hitler is based on three arguments. First, nobody else had ever advocated systematic killing by the state as a way to solve the Jewish question. That Hitler had done so in the 1920s is not in itself proof that he acted accordingly in the 1940s. But it is a strong indication if taken together with his programmatic consistency in foreign policy and with the position of absolute authority he had acquired in Germany since 1933.

Second, all participants who expressed themselves on the subject testified both during and after the war that the killings were ordered by Hitler. Not one of them has ever suggested that somebody else proposed or initiated them. The widespread assertion that Himmler was the principal driving force is clearly refuted by contemporary evidence. Even if all the postwar testimonies are dismissed as apologetic, the wartime statements are convincing enough.

Third, given the nature of the Nazi state and its ruler, it is difficult to imagine that an act of such scope with such far-reaching consequences, one so compromising, moreover, to the conduct of the war and the chances for victory, should have been initiated by subordinate agencies. Since there is no other case of this kind, it can safely be ruled out.

If, then, we agree that the decision was made by Hitler, we must ask how it was reached and transmitted. I have already eliminated the possibility that a single order was given at a certain date. It is strange that this should ever have been imagined. It is in clear contradiction to most comparable practice and can perhaps be explained only by an arresting horror at crimes unprecedented in human history that has, for a long time, prevented or paralyzed conventional historical research and understanding. In other words, to suppose that Hitler had one day called a conference and given an order to exterminate the Jews, and that this order had been carried

out, is totally unrealistic. It is as if we had forgotten everything we know about decision making. Never has an act of
such magnitude as the Holocaust been decided upon in one
conference and by one order alone. If we take for compari-
son's sake Hitler's decision to attack the Soviet Union, we can
easily trace the process over many months or even years.

After decades of pondering the project and of interior and
exterior preparations, Hitler informed his generals on July
31, 1940, of his resolve *(Entschluss)* to attack in the spring of
1941. Then military preparations began. A first operational
draft of the general staff was ready on August 5, 1940. On
November 12 instructions were given to continue all preparations that had been ordered orally. On December 18 the directive for Operation Barbarossa was issued. On May 1, 1941,
the date for launching the offensive was set for June 22. The
final order to attack was given by Hitler on June 17.

The fact that we do not have comparable documentary
evidence for the preparation of the Holocaust must not lead
us to suppose that this process was shorter. But it may well
have been different. Although an unprovoked war of conquest
was unusual, Hitler could feel that it was justified by historical experience and assume that a suitable pretext could be
found when the time came. Moreover, once he had succeeded
in convincing his generals of the necessity and the feasibility
of the war, the campaign was, in its military aspect, a conventional operation that could be prepared and conducted with
the aid of the traditional instrument of the general staff. After
all, wars had been waged since time immemorial.

The mass slaughter of unarmed men, women, and children,
however, was quite a different matter. Neither a convincing
justification nor a pretext could be found easily. There were
no preexisting organizational or technical instruments to fall
back on. As Christopher Browning noted, the Nazis were
venturing into uncharted territory and attempting the un-

precedented; they had no maps to follow.[64] Martin Broszat pointed out that the extremely illegal character of the killings sufficed to preclude a written order by the head of state.[65]

But these were not the only difficulties. After Hitler had encountered the protest, particularly by the churches but also from within the party, against the killing of the insane he had to expect a similar protest; certainly he could not assume that almost none would arise. Still more important, he could not assume that all his supporters would follow him along the road to the Holocaust. A striking example of what he could expect came from Gauleiter Wilhelm Kube. An old hand at Jew baiting, Kube was confronted with the bloody reality at his post as commissar general in Minsk; he was appalled at such actions and protested against them.[66] Hitler knew his men well enough to fear such reactions.

The next difficulty was in logistics. In this area as well, the lack of documentary evidence limits our understanding. Nevertheless, in the case of the Nisko operation of October 1939, when Eichmann dispatched two transports of 912 and 672 Jews from Vienna, we can follow in exceptional detail the extent of difficulties involved.[67] Through this case it may be easier to recognize the problems that could arise in transporting millions to places where they could be killed. The notion that even Hitler, wielding such immense power as he did, could restrict himself to issuing just one order to this effect is incomprehensible.

Another difficulty was of a technical nature. There certainly was experience to be derived from the killing of the insane in gas chambers. It requires further study to test the hypothesis of some scholars that this program was perhaps devised as a preparatory stage to the final solution. They argue that this action was stopped in August 1941 not only, as is usually believed, because of the public protest but also because the personnel and the equipment involved were to be used for the final solution. However this may have been, it can easily be seen from the improvisation of killing methods after June 1941 that the technical question was far from having been solved by then.

The enormous difficulties facing the implementation of the final solution should suffice to explain the lack of coherence in its execution. There is no need to draw the conclusion that it was the spontaneous result of situations that had developed. Could it not have been in Hitler's interest or been his intention to create the situational confusion in order to overcome the difficulties involved? Whether this was the case or not, the difficulties suggest a departure from our conventional notions of how decisions are made and orders issued.

In this respect we must now include in our consideration what we said earlier about the ambiguity of Hitler's anti-Semitism. That was the principal and most fundamental difficulty. His desire to exterminate the Jews was in conflict with his desire to win the war. He was just as unable to set his priorities when preparing the Holocaust as he had been when he had formulated his goals in the 1920s. As we have seen, Göring seems to have recognized the problem when he said that it was more important to win the war than to implement racial policy. Hitler was unable to understand this view and still tried to demonstrate that the Holocaust did not compromise the chances of victory. This inability also and most basically contributes to explaining the lack of coherence in his policy.

There is further evidence of this in the later course of events. In 1942 Hitler's task became easier as the course of the war began to set his priorities for him. On November 8 he said in a public speech in Munich:

You will recall the session of the Reichstag during which I declared: If Jewry should imagine that it could bring about an international world war to exterminate the European races, the result will not be the extermination of the European races, but the extermination of Jewry in Europe. People always laughed about me as a prophet. Of those who laughed then, countless numbers no longer laugh today, and those who still laugh now will perhaps no longer laugh a short time from now. This realization will spread beyond Europe throughout the entire world. International Jewry will be recognized in its full demonic peril; we National Socialists will see to that.[68]

It should first be noted that Hitler used the formulation "international world war" as he had earlier, on September 30 of that year. This pleonasm was, of course, ridiculous unless Hitler wanted to differentiate between a national world war for living space and an international world war against the Jews. This may indeed have been his intention.

Furthermore, we must remember that in the course of that autumn of 1942 the second assault against the Soviet Union had failed, like the first, and the American invasion of North Africa had just begun. Yet according to Hitler's earlier plans, Russia was to have been vanquished by 1941, before the United States was ready for war. Thus there were definite reasons for Hitler to wonder if the war perhaps could not be won. Hitler would, of course, not admit this in public. But he may have felt that if he could not acquire new living space for Germany, he might at least achieve something for humanity. As the fortunes of war turned against Germany, Hitler became more and more convinced that the destruction of the Jews was his gift to the world. This became totally clear toward the end of the war. In a dictated memoir on February 13, 1945, Hitler said, "I have lanced the Jewish abscess, like the others. For this, the future will be eternally grateful to us." And again in his last words recorded on April 2 in his bunker in Berlin, "The world will be eternally grateful to National Socialism that I have eradicated the Jews in Germany and Central Europe."[69]

For the last time we return to the question how and when the decision was made. There can no longer be a reasonable doubt that it was made by Hitler. But how are we to envision the process by which he made it? It seems that, first of all, we have to abandon our conventional notion of orders. In view of the tremendous difficulties to be overcome, this was not an undertaking that simply could be ordered, not even within the framework of a dictatorship. Years of persistent effort were required by Hitler to bring his collaborators—more the high-ranking functionaries than the henchmen—around to his idea and to lead them patiently into carrying out his plan.

He had to intensify the anti-Jewish feelings of most of his collaborators to a degree that the urge became strong enough among them to get rid of the Jews. He had then to show or to let it appear that the elimination could not be achieved by emigration, evacuation, or deportation. He had to present the Russian Jews as a potential source of resistance to German rule. After he had succeeded in this, he could suggest killing the unwanted Polish and German Jews, and after that had proved feasible he could include the West European Jews. He may have made vague suggestions here and there, both in public and within his inner circle, to various collaborators who were competing against each other for his favor. He may have held out prospects of promotion. He may have flattered or threatened, appealing to loyalty, giving or taking, playing one supporter against the other, according to the acquired art of ruling by his system of government.

Viewed from this perspective, we may date certain intimations, instructions, directives, and orders if it is understood that these were not always clearly defined. For example, after the pogrom of November 1938, when Goebbels was criticized by Göring for the economic damage incurred, Hitler had a long conversation with Göring after which the idea permeated the inner circle that there would be a drastic solution to the Jewish problem when war came. It was first expressed by Göring on November 12, a fortnight later in the SS newspaper, and finally by Hitler himself in his famous prophecy. Is it not reasonable to assume that Hitler had said something of the sort to Göring, then waited for reactions and, when they proved encouraging, promoted the idea in public?

Or consider this recollection by Himmler's masseur, Felix Kersten. Immediately after the French campaign Himmler was summoned by Hitler and told that he would have to carry out the extermination of the European Jews.[70] Admittedly, Kersten is unreliable. But is it not suggestive that Hitler in those days, when he was planning the war against Russia, should have thought of the final solution as well? We must regard this, not as an order, but as yet another step along the way.

Certainly Hitler must have given an order in the spring of 1941 providing Himmler with special powers to kill Russian Jews. But at first Hitler's order may well have been only to kill Jewish party and state officials in the USSR and to incite pogroms there. When this plan was well underway, with the campaign running according to plan, Hitler may have extended the order in July or August to cover all other Russian Jews and included the German Jews as well. In other words, he may have tested the ground first and then have proceeded gradually.

Once more it is important to recognize that he did not assign the task to a single agency, the SS and police, but to his personal chancellery as well, which had carried out the killing of the insane. Both agencies were later to compete. This fits in perfectly with the nature of his rule: the gradual disclosure of his objectives and the competition of agencies.

It has not and could not have been my aim to date the entire decision-making process. For the requisite research is in its very beginnings. But it was my aim to suggest how the orders may have been given, how we should envision the decision-making process, and how more confirmation can be achieved. It appears to me that our perspective must be changed. We must, above all, never isolate the Holocaust either from Hitler's thinking or from the difficult conditions under which he acted. We must not overlook, in other words, the ambiguity of his racial program and the difficulties of its implementation. Awareness of that ambiguity and those difficulties may lead not to an understanding, which is probably beyond our reach, but at least to a clarification, which in my view we owe not merely to historical scholarship but above all to the victims.

4

Hitler Challenges America

On Thursday, December 11, 1941, at 2:18 P.M. Ribbentrop, the German foreign minister, received the American chargé d'affaires (the ambassador had been recalled after the anti-Jewish pogrom of November 1938) in his Berlin office on the Wilhelmstrasse and, standing, read a statement to him that concluded with the declaration that Germany regarded itself "as being at war with the United States of America as of today." The meeting lasted three minutes.[1] At 3:00 P.M. the German Reichstag met to hear a speech by Hitler in which he announced the declaration of war.[2] While he was speaking, the German chargé d'affaires in Washington at 9:30 A.M. local time delivered a note to the State Department worded identically with the statement read by Ribbentrop.[3] Thus the two countries were at war with each other for the second time in their history. Whereas it was the United States that had declared war in 1917, in 1941 the declaration of war was made by Germany.

More than forty years later it is still unclear what prompted the German government to take this step. Indeed it does not seem easy to say why, when the German campaign against the Soviet Union was stuck in the snow in front of Moscow and when Britain was still undefeated, Germany should take on as an additional enemy the very power to whom it had succumbed in World War I. It has become customary, therefore, to assume that there is no convincing explanation for this decision, that it did not serve the interests of the German ruling circles, that it followed the Japanese attack on Pearl Harbor as a more or less impulsive expression of desperation or megalomania, or even that it is a sign that Hitler almost wanted to bring about his own downfall. Whatever reasons are given for it, and though most of the relevant documents have been accessible for some time, the decision remains puzzling.

Since the decision was made by Hitler, incidentally without any consultation with his military advisers, we must once more begin with him, with his conduct of foreign policy and with his assessment of the situation in 1941. In particular the decision-making process must be retraced as precisely as possible, and so the inquiry will become largely a piece of diplomatic history.

Hitler's foreign policy followed a plan already laid down in the 1920s.[4] Since I have dealt with it in some detail in Chapter 2, I shall restrict myself to the points relevant to our present question. It will be remembered that Hitler's main aim in foreign policy was a war of conquest against the Soviet Union. When Hitler reflected on how this war was to be won, his thoughts were from the beginning not really directed toward the actual opponent, for the Soviet Union was supposed to collapse swiftly under a German attack. Rather, his thoughts were directed toward establishing a diplomatic constellation in which Germany could not be prevented by other powers from achieving success. In Hitler's eyes their intervention was the real problem, not Russian resistance.

What had to be avoided was a coalition against Germany such as had existed in World War I, resulting in a war on several fronts that the country was too weak to win. Thus Hitler envisaged a series of precautionary measures to protect Germany. First, Italy and Britain were to be persuaded by means of concessions to tolerate German expansion. Then France was to be defeated in a preliminary war before the war of conquest against Russia was begun. Originally other powers such as the United States or Japan seemed too remote to require attention.

Although Hitler managed to conclude an agreement with Italy, he failed to reach one with Britain. This failure led Hitler to include Japan in his plans for the first time. His dealings with Japan were intended to shift British attention from Europe to East Asia. If an alliance could be brought about with Japan, which was menacing British Far Eastern positions, while the alliance with Italy threatened Britain in the Mediterranean, then the combination of alliances against Britain might be so powerful that England would finally prefer to accept a settlement granting Germany a free hand on the continent. Behind the screen of ideological propaganda, this was the real purpose of the Anti-Comintern Pact concluded with Japan in 1936 and joined by Italy in 1937. The effort failed, however. Britain entered the war together with France on September 3, 1939. Hitler then hoped that Britain would give in when it had lost its French ally and had been driven militarily from the continent. The western campaign of 1940 was intended to serve the dual purpose of defeating France and discouraging Britain. Again Hitler's stratagem failed. France was defeated, but Britain held out.

Nevertheless Hitler decided after the fall of France to attack the Soviet Union in May 1941 and to defeat it within five months. In the prevailing circumstances the eastern campaign was also to serve a dual purpose. It was meant to lead to the conquest of living space as well as to discourage Britain once and for all. Now the United States came into the picture for the first time along with, once again, Japan.

Britain's hope, Hitler argued to his generals on July 31, 1940, lies with Russia and America. If and when the Russian hope vanishes, the American hope will vanish as well, because the fall of Russia will upgrade Japan in East Asia on a tremendous scale. This argument was partially meant by Hitler to convince his generals of the necessity and the feasibility of the Russian campaign. But in part it was also his real reasoning. The first and overriding purpose of the Russian campaign was conquest, but the second and subordinate purpose was to end the war with Britain. With the expected defeat of Russia, Britain's last hope would be obliterated. America would not intervene if Japan were pursuing an active policy in East Asia as a result of the German victory over the Soviet Union. Even if Britain still held out it would not matter, for with the conquest of Russia Germany would acquire an economic and strategic base from which it could carry on the war indefinitely.

During the preparations for the eastern campaign Hitler's reasoning followed this line quite consistently. He was not much concerned about Russia, which he still thought would collapse quickly. What he did worry about was the other powers, which could hinder Germany or assist the Soviet Union. This danger increased the longer the campaign lasted. If against his expectations the conquest of Russia could not be completed in the course of 1941, British and American operations of various kinds were to be feared. In fact the United States was already giving increasing support to the British war effort. Both powers, however, could be engaged by Japan in East Asia and thus be distracted from Europe and deterred from intervening there.

This was, for Hitler, the purpose of the Tripartite Pact concluded by Germany, Italy, and Japan on September 27, 1940, which stated that the three powers would support each other with any and all means should one of them be attacked by the United States.[5] It thus guaranteed that if America entered the war, it would have to fight on two fronts, in the Atlantic as well as in the Pacific; thus Germany would not have to fear undivided American intervention as in World War I. Hitler's interest in the Tripartite Pact clearly was to prevent the United States from entering the war on the side of Britain.

This deterrence, however, was not sufficient for Hitler. In order to gain additional security he urged Japan to attack British positions in East Asia. During a high-level discussion of the plans of attack against the Soviet Union, he said on February 15, 1941, "It must be Germany's aim to make Japan act as soon as possible in the Far East. It must gain possession of Singapore and all the raw material areas it needs for the continuation of the war, especially if America should intervene."[6] In a directive on cooperation with Japan dated March 5 he repeated these thoughts, adding that "strong English forces will be tied down and the focus of American interest will be diverted to the Pacific."[7]

Japan did not follow Hitler's suggestion. Instead, in the spring of 1941 Japan opened negotiations with the United States, which had opposed Japanese penetration into China and Indochina with various measures.[8] If these talks were to lead to an agreement, a Japanese attack on Singapore would become even less likely and America would again be completely free to act in Europe, especially if Japan denounced the Tripartite Pact or obviously failed to abide by it. In view of this threat, Hitler enlarged on his guarantee to Japan under the Tripartite Pact. When the Japanese foreign minister Matsuoka paid a visit to Berlin and Rome in March and April 1941, Hitler promised him that Germany would join Japan immediately and unconditionally in case of a Japanese conflict with either America or Russia.[9] Whereas under the Tripartite Pact Germany was obliged to assist Japan only in the case of an American attack, Hitler had now included by implication the case of a Japanese attack as well and had added Russia to the list. But Matsuoka did not pay much attention and may not even have fully understood what Hitler was saying.

During these talks the Germans not only repeated insistently that the Japanese should attack Singapore. They also made more or less veiled hints that a German-Soviet war was imminent. Once more, however, Matsuoka did not grasp what he was told. On his way back to Japan he concluded a neutrality pact with the Soviet Union in Moscow and told the American ambassador there that the Germans apparently had wanted their hints to be transmitted to Stalin to induce him to increase Russian exports.[10]

It is true that neither Hitler nor Ribbentrop had been outspoken with Matsuoka on this point, and this was again consistent with their policy. At first sight it must certainly have seemed tempting to persuade Japan to participate in the upcoming eastern war. If the Soviet Union were attacked from the west and the east simultaneously, its chances of survival would be even lower than they were already considered to be. But in fact this line of consideration was only of secondary importance to Hitler, just as it had always been. The military aspect of the Russian campaign was not his concern. His primary goal was still to persuade Japan to attack Britain in East Asia and thus indirectly to deter America from intervention in Europe. It was only because Japan appeared to be hesitating that Hitler extended his promises of support in order to persuade Japan to enter the war, whether against Britain, as he would have preferred, or against Russia or even America, which still seemed least desirable.

Overall this order of preference did not change during the following weeks. The Japanese ambassador in Berlin, Oshima, was repeatedly given hints that the war was approaching, and he reported on April 16 and again in the first days of June that he had gained the impression that Japanese participation in

Germany's eastern war was perhaps desired after all. It seems that Ribbentrop was more keen on such participation than Hitler. But even he told Oshima clearly what the German position was on June 4: "It would, of course, be up to Japan to act as it saw fit, but Japan's cooperation in the fight against the Soviet Union would be welcomed *if* the [Japanese] advance to the south should run into difficulty because of supplies and equipment [my italics]."[11]

It was precisely this position that Weizsäcker, the well-informed secretary of state in the Foreign Office, noted in his diary on June 8: "Now that [Oshima] has been told more clearly or it has become clearer to him that the Russian question is becoming acute, he appears to want to see to it that Japan will move on if not to Singapore then at least toward Vladivostok."[12] If not Singapore, then at least Vladivostok: That was still the order of preference, and provoking America's entry into the war was still Hitler's last choice. Japan was not to attack America and Germany was to avoid any sort of provocation. On the eve of the war, on June 21, Hitler made this clear to the navy once more. As Admiral Raeder noted, "Until the effects of 'Barbarossa' [the code word for the Russian campaign] can be seen, i.e., for several weeks, the führer wants every possible incident with the U.S.A. to be strictly avoided."[13]

The following day, June 22, 1941, several weeks later than originally planned because of the Balkan campaign, Germany invaded the Soviet Union. In Japan Matsuoka advocated Japan's immediate participation, but he could not gain sufficient support and resigned on July 16.[14] In Germany Ribbentrop, worried additionally over the continuing Japanese-American negotiations, now pressed vigorously for Japan to enter the war against Russia. He spoke to Oshima on this, and on June 28 he sent the following directive to his ambassador in Tokyo: An advance to the South toward Singapore was and would remain of great importance. Since Japan was not yet prepared for it at the moment, however, it should advance against Soviet Russia without delay. "In this way it would also free its rear for the advance to the South." Then followed the old German reasoning: "It can be assumed that a rapid defeat of Soviet Russia, especially if Japan participates from the east, will be the best means of convincing the United States that it would be totally pointless to enter into war on the side of a then completely isolated England opposed by the most powerful combination in the world."[15] This directive demonstrates once more that Japan's entry into the war was still desired primarily to deter the United States and only secondarily as military assistance against the Soviet Union, which Germany at that time believed itself able to defeat alone.

This position was confirmed when American forces occupied Iceland on July 7. Understandably the German navy was extremely concerned about this move, since they saw in it a serious hindrance to their own warfare in the Atlantic. Yet when Admiral Raeder asked Hitler two days later for a "political decision" on whether the occupation of Iceland should be considered America's entry into the war or an act of provocation to be ignored, he was told "that it was of utmost importance to [Hitler] to delay America's entry into the war for another one or two months, since on the one hand the entire air force was needed for the eastern campaign and on the other a success of the eastern campaign would have a tremendous effect on the overall situation and probably also on the attitude of the United States." Hitler wanted, therefore, "any incident to be avoided as before."[16]

Meanwhile Japan was still hesitating and negotiating in Washington. Ribbentrop now suspected Japan of attempting on its side exactly what Germany wanted to achieve for itself. On July 10 he anxiously asked his ambassador in Tokyo whether there might be an interest in Japan in reaching an agreement with America so that America would then get embroiled in the European war and Japan, without coming into open conflict with America, would have a free hand in East Asia to settle the Chinese affair and expand further to the south. All the more urgently he requested Ambassador Ott "to persuade Japan to enter the war against Russia as quickly as possible."[17]

Recognizing the danger in this situation, Hitler stepped in once again and received Oshima in his headquarters on July 14. "If we can keep the United States out of the war at all," he said, "we will only be able to do so by destroying Russia and only if Japan and Germany act simultaneously and unequivocally."[18] Fear of American intervention and the desire to keep America out of the war were still the cornerstones of Germany's Japanese policy. They remained so even when America sided more and more openly with Britain and also supported the Soviet Union.

In August President Roosevelt and Prime Minister Churchill met and proclaimed the Atlantic Charter, which referred to "the final destruction of the Nazi tyranny"—strong words indeed from a neutral country. In September Roosevelt ordered the policy of "shoot on sight" against Axis ships in the Atlantic and explained the policy in an unusually solemn radio broadcast. Such a deliberate provocation would have justified a German declaration of war or at least the announcement of identical retaliatory measures.

Yet even then Hitler demanded restraint. After Raeder had explained the new situation in the Atlantic to him on September 17, he recorded the result of the conversation as follows: "On the basis of a thorough examination of the overall situation (end September great decision in the Russian campaign), the führer has asked to see to it that there will be no incidents in the merchant war until about the middle of [October]." Contrary orders that had already been prepared for German submarines were withdrawn.[19]

At the same time the German leaders were growing more and more suspicious of Japan, which was still negotiating with America. Hitler no longer wanted to insist on Japan's entry into the war "so as not to create the impression that we need the Japanese."[20] On September 13 Ribbentrop even notified the Japanese government that Roosevelt's aggressive policy was bound to lead to a state of war between Germany and Italy on the one side and America on the other, and that by the terms of the Tripartite Pact this would necessitate Japan's immediate entry into the war against America. He insisted that Japan transmit a declaration to this effect to Washington.[21] Japan was expected at least to help prevent an American entry into the war. It was also warned that its negotiations might soon become pointless because it would have to fulfill its pledge of support according to the Tripartite Pact.

The month of October passed without visible change in the Japanese attitude. Ambassador Ott reported "a certain helplessness as to the course to be pursued" and the increasing feeling that a conflict with the United States was unavoidable.[22] On October 20 he reported in a cable that in the new cabinet under Tōjō, which had come into office on October 18, the forces working toward an agreement with America were now weak.[23] But on October 31, after a meeting with the new foreign minister, Tōgō, he could only report that a decision had not yet been reached about the warning to the United States requested by Germany on September 13.[24] The Germans took no further initiative.

Then at last signs came from Japan. On November 5 Ambassador Ott reported "with reservation" a "cautious approach on the part of the [Japanese] navy concerning a German assurance not to conclude a separate peace or armistice in case of a Japanese-American war."[25] On November 18 he reported that the head of the section for foreign armies of the Japanese general staff, General Okamoto, had "apparently on higher instruction" mentioned the following point to the German military attaché with the request that it be passed on. Okamoto said:

The sending of Kurusu [who had been sent additionally to the negotiations in Washington early in November] represents a last attempt to clear up Japanese-American relations. The Japanese general staff does not expect a peaceful solution to be possible. The Japanese self-help then necessary is likely to be followed by the entry of the United States into war. . . . The Japanese general staff thinks that mutual assistance can best be assured by a commitment of both states, Germany and Japan, to conclude an armistice or peace not separately but only together.[26]

This was a strange request by the Japanese. Apparently the Japanese general staff was not aware that Hitler had long ago given a much more extended pledge to join Japan in a war with the United States immediately and unconditionally. Instead of referring to this assurance now, Japan was asking only that the two states not end their wars separately. Since Germany was not at war with America, this could only apply to Britain and Russia, with which Japan was not at war. Japan obviously wanted a protective distraction in Europe similar to that which Germany had been seeking for a long time in East Asia.

Ott's telegram reached Berlin on November 19. Without much delay Ribbentrop replied on the twenty-first that the ambassador himself or the military attaché should tell General Okamoto that they had reported to Berlin "and heard that there the idea of concluding an armistice or peace only jointly in case, for whatever reason, Japan or Germany were to become involved in a war with the Unites States was taken for granted and that Germany was perfectly willing to spell it out in an agreement."[27] That was a cautious answer to an exploratory question. Yet Ribbentrop had at once included the case of a German-American state of war as well and had suggested a formal agreement.

Ott answered quickly on November 23. He had at first had the military attaché carry out Ribbentrop's instructions, but had then received Okamoto at Okamoto's request and Okamoto had brought thanks from Tōjō. Thus the highest level had been reached. Okamoto had said that "he was pleased to receive confirmation once more that Germany would not abandon Japan in case of a conflict with the United States." Then Ott went on reporting: "He [Okamoto] requested me to inform him whether it was my opinion that Germany would also consider itself to be at war with the United States if Japan were to open hostilities [*im Falle einer japanischen Kriegseröffnung*]." [28]

Now the Japanese had gone one step further. Obviously encouraged by Ribbentrop's positive reply, they now wanted to know if Germany was prepared to join Japan in a war against America. Okamoto spoke clearly of the Japanese opening hostilities, since he apparently was well aware that the opposite case of an American initiative was covered by the Tripartite Pact. But he did not say whether Japan on its side would join Germany in a war against America and he did not refer to Hitler's assurance given in April, which appeared to be unknown even to the Japanese government. He asked (that was the meaning behind his words) whether Germany would enter a war against America started by Japan even though it was not obliged by the pact to do so.

Thus the decisive question had been raised. Certainly Hitler must have been relieved that Japan was finally acting. But at the same time he was now confronted with the prospect of a war against America, which he had tried to avoid by every means available. In fact we know, although Ribbentrop could not have known, that Japan's supreme decision-making body, the Liaison Conference between the government and the armed forces, had decided on November 12 that Germany and Italy should be informed if war with America became inevitable and that the following agreement should be negotiated: "(a) The participation of Germany (Italy) in the war against the United States; (b) Neither of the two parties will make peace separately." In his exploratory approach Okamoto had asked about these two points in reverse order. In the Japanese minutes an important note follows: "In case Germany demands that we participate in the war against the Soviet Union, we will respond that we do not intend to join the war for the time being. If this should lead to a situation whereby Germany will delay her entry into the war against the United States, it cannot be helped."[29]

Ott's telegram containing Okamoto's decisive question arrived in Berlin on November 24 at 3:00 A.M. There is no indication that Ribbentrop ever replied to it. His next telegram in the publication of the German Foreign Office documents is dated December 6, by which time the agreement between Germany, Italy, and Japan had already been drafted. There are large gaps in the German records for these crucial days, probably because of the destruction shortly before the end of the war. The relevant Japanese records also seem to have been almost totally destroyed in 1945. Fortunately, the gaps can be filled to a certain extent by numerous diplomatic messages exchanged between Tokyo and the Japanese embassies in Europe that were intercepted and decoded by American and British intelligence services; these have recently been published in full in a collection called The "Magic" Background of Pearl Harbor.[30]

Nevertheless, a detailed reconstruction of the decision-making process in Germany at this time is difficult. Furthermore, the decisive conversations between Hitler and Ribbentrop were not recorded in any manner, and we cannot look into Hitler's and Ribbentrop's tormented minds during these days when the Russian campaign ran into its most serious crisis. On the other hand, the result of their reflections is clear. The decisive question confronting Hitler was whether Germany should promise to join Japan in a war started by Japan against the United States. I think we can safely assume that he was immediately informed about Okamoto's question. Ribbentrop had probably transmitted Ott's telegram to him. Besides Hitler came to Berlin for three days on November 27 to celebrate the renewal of the Anti-Comintern Pact. Hitler and Ribbentrop together received the representatives of their allies during these days. They thus had ample opportunity to exchange views.

But a decision may not have been reached then. No reply was sent to Ott, and no directive was issued as far as we know. On the evening of November 28, four days after the arrival of Ott's telegram, Ribbentrop received Oshima, the Japanese ambassador in Berlin. According to the German minutes, which are not complete but record a large part of the conversation short of the conclusion, neither Oshima nor Ribbentrop mentioned Okamoto's question.[31] Among many other things, they talked about the possibility of a Japanese-American war. Ribbentrop, saying that the conflict was inevitable, recommended that Japan not hesitate "to tackle the Americans today." But at least in the recorded first part of the conversation he did not say, and Oshima did not ask, how Germany would react in such a case. A different interpretation is presented in a telegram sent by Oshima to Tokyo on the next day and intercepted by the American intelligence service.[32] According to this text Ribbentrop declared at the end of the conversation, "Should Japan become engaged in a war with the United States, Germany, of course, would join the war immediately. There is absolutely no possibility of Germany's entering into a separate peace with the United States under such circumstances. The führer is determined on that point."

There is no reason to doubt that Oshima was able to understand what he was told and that he informed his government correctly. This then would mean that Okamoto's question had been given a clear answer, and the two states would have been able to begin formulating the terms of their agreement. In reality, however, they did not do so at once. Further decisions had to be made in Tokyo. But when they were made and transmitted to Ribbentrop by Oshima in the evening of December 1, the foreign minister told the ambassador that he had to consult Hitler but could not reach him until December 4 or 5.[33] This is not quite compatible with the assumption derived from Oshima's telegram that the decision had already been made by November 28. But since the Japanese were now demanding a formal agreement, Ribbentrop may have felt that he had to consult Hitler once more. We must also consider that the Germans had not been told how imminent the Pacific war was.

At first sight it seems unlikely that on such an important question the German foreign minister should not have been able to contact his führer for three or four days. Yet it is true that on December 2 Hitler flew to the south of the eastern front at Taganrog, that he planned to return to his headquarters near Rastenburg in East Prussia, but he was hindered by bad weather, had to spend the night in Poltava on the return flight, and so did not arrive at his headquarters until December 4.[34] There is even some evidence for Ribbentrop's improbable statement that he was not able to get in touch with Hitler at this time. Hitler's valet, Heinz Linge, who was also on the flight, related after the war that in Poltava Hitler "suffered excruciatingly at the thought of what might be happening at headquarters and in his chancellery while he was hundreds of kilometers away, cut off from the outside world, without communications, imprisoned in an old tumbledown and bug-ridden castle."[35] This seems the more likely, since during these days the crisis on the eastern front was accompanied by a serious crisis in the supreme command of the army.

Hitler took off from Poltava on December 4 and returned to his East Prussian headquarters in the course of the day. There Ribbentrop must have finally been able to reach him. Whereas it had originally been assumed that Ribbentrop spoke to him by telephone, it now seems clear, according to another intercepted Japanese telegram, that he went there in person.[36] This corroborates our former assumption that a final decision had not been reached on November 28 and was not made until the afternoon of December 4.

This is confirmed again by the German records. In the course of that evening, at 9:30 P.M., the German ambassador in Rome, Mackensen, was phoned from Berlin by order of Ribbentrop and forewarned that in the next few hours he would receive instructions by telephone that he would have to carry out during the night in the presence of Ciano, the Italian foreign minister, and if necessary the duce himself. The instructions reached Rome at 1:30 A.M. on December 5 and "were not coded." Having received the full text, Mackensen went at 2:20 A.M. to Ciano's residence and read him "the German text orally translated into Italian," since there had been no time to produce a written translation. Ciano immediately gave the Italian consent, which was communicated to Berlin at 2:45 A.M., so that by 4:00 A.M. the Japanese ambassador could be given the text approved by both Axis powers and send it on to Tokyo.[37]

What had apparently been drawn up and agreed to in extreme haste during this night was the draft of a new tripartite agreement.[38] Its first article stated that if war should break out between any one of the partners and the United States, the other two would at once consider themselves at war with the United States as well. The second article stipulated that the three partners would in case of war not conclude an armistice or peace with either America or England except by complete mutual consent. According to the third article the agreement was to be kept strictly secret, but the obligation contained in Article 2 was to be published in a form to be agreed upon as soon as the war had begun.

Thus Hitler promised Japan to join immediately in a war against America regardless of how it came about. But he had made certain that Japan gave the same pledge as far as Germany was concerned. This had been added to the original

Japanese draft at Germany's request. Ciano immediately stressed this when he said that it appeared to him to be an agreeable emendation "in our favor."[39] In the same vein Weizsäcker noted on December 6, "I think that we cannot refuse [the Japanese request] but must demand reciprocity in point 2 [entry into war]. The negotiations were conducted in this sense. I expect us to reach a conclusion today."[40]

The agreement was not signed. While details were still being thrashed out in telegrams exchanged between Tokyo and Berlin, the Japanese attacked Pearl Harbor on December 7. The attack became known in Berlin on the evening of that Sunday. It dramatically dispelled German doubts about whether Japan really would enter the war. If this had been the goal of the German promise, it was now achieved and Hitler was free again to join Japan or not. Moreover, since his aim had been to involve the United States in the Pacific and thus reduce the danger of American intervention in Europe, this involvement was now an established fact and Hitler might have wondered whether a German declaration of war was still necessary. At any rate, it did not follow "at once," as had been provided for in the now obsolete draft agreement. Instead the partners began immediately to negotiate a new agreement. On Monday, December 8 Ribbentrop gave Oshima a draft and sent it in the evening to Ott in Tokyo with the request to urge acceptance quickly enough for it to be signed in Berlin on Wednesday morning at the latest, because it was, he added, "possibly to be made public in a special form."[41]

This referred to the meeting of the Reichstag, which apparently had already been decided upon. Hitler came to Berlin on Tuesday morning to prepare for it.[42] On the same day he ordered all restrictions on naval warfare to be abolished and the United States "to be now regarded as an enemy."[43] There can be no doubt that the German declaration of war had been decided upon and the haste of this decision is explained by the fear that the Americans would steal the show. (Roosevelt, incidentally, had no reason to ask the still reluctant Congress for a declaration of war; he was fully informed by the intercepted messages of what was going on between Berlin and Tokyo.)

These negotiations lasted longer than Ribbentrop wanted. The Japanese insisted on supplementing the agreement with some explanatory additions, which did not reach Berlin until Tuesday night. Ribbentrop gave his consent on Wednesday and once again requested a quick response so that the authorization for Oshima to sign the treaty would arrive at the latest by noon on Wednesday.[44] In the meantime everything had been prepared in Berlin for the ceremony and the German chargé d'affaires in Washington had already been instructed to deliver the declaration of war on Thursday.[45] Oshima finally received his authorization, whereupon the agreement was signed by Ribbentrop, by the Italian ambassador Alfieri, and by Oshima on Thursday, December 11, presumably just before the declaration of war was made. On the same afternoon Hitler announced the agreement at the end of his long speech to the Reichstag by reading it out word for word.

Unlike the first agreement, the second one did not contain an obligation to go to war, since this was now a foregone conclusion. The agreement stipulated only the obligation not to conclude an armistice or a peace treaty with the United States or England without complete mutual consent. It therefore came to be called unofficially the no-separate-peace treaty (*Nichtsonderfriedensvertrag*).[46]

Let us now return to the question we raised at the outset: Why did Germany declare war on the United States on December 11, 1941? We have to state first that the answer remains tentative, but our assumptions now rest on firmer ground. Contrary to what is commonly believed, the decision to declare war was not prompted by the Japanese attack on Pearl Harbor. The decision had been preceded by short but determined negotiations between Germany and Japan, and it had largely been made in the course of those negotiations at a time when Hitler was not yet completely certain that Japan would really enter the war.

For a long time Hitler had wanted to avoid war with the United States. He had done so even after Roosevelt's "shoot on sight" order of September 1941, which could have served as a plausible pretext for a declaration of war. In the German note and in Hitler's speech of December 11 this "shoot on sight" order was certainly mentioned as one of the reasons for the declaration of war, but it can be ruled out as the real or only reason. In fact, in his speech Hitler did not deny that his decision was primarily connected with Japan's policy, which undoubtedly was the central factor in his decision making.

In order to keep America out of the war, he had constantly sought since the spring of 1941 that Japan would enter it, preferably against Britain or, failing that, against the Soviet Union. Only his concern that Japan might not undertake either course prompted him in April to promise Matsuoka that Germany would also join Japan in a war against America. Thus the simple explanation could be given that Hitler remained consistent and carried out in December what he had promised in April. To a large extent this explanation seems to be convincing, but it is not altogether sufficient. The situation in December was dramatically different from that in April. In the meantime it had become obvious that contrary to Hitler's expectations of the spring, the Soviet Union could not be defeated in 1941 and perhaps not in 1942 either. In view of this severe military crisis it could well be asked whether it was still in Germany's interest to follow Japan into its war against America.

Ribbentrop may have thought so. This would explain why he did not answer General Okamoto's question of November 23 until the Japanese returned to it urgently, and why he then wanted to discuss the matter once more with Hitler. It is not certain whether he could not get in touch with him for technical reasons. He may have preferred a personal conversation to a telephone call or radio contact, giving him greater freedom to explain his misgivings. There are indications in Weizsäcker's diary that Ribbentrop particularly wanted to avoid the obligation not to make peace separately, since it would exclude a separate peace with Britain.[47]

However this may have been, Hitler decided probably on November 28 and definitely by December 4 to meet the Japanese request. But now the Germans were not satisfied with the exchange of simple promises with which the Japanese would have been content. The Germans demanded a formal agreement based on reciprocity. They apparently thought it possible that a German-American war could come sooner than one between Japan and America. When this war came on December 7, the agreement had not yet become effective, so once more a decision had to be made. Hitler could have avoided a declaration of war on formal grounds, particularly because the advantage he had been seeking, namely, the reduction of the danger of American intervention in Europe, was now won in his view. He could also have declined the Japanese request to enter the war against America in the same way that Japan had declined the German request to enter the war against Russia. He could even make his earlier request a condition of Germany's meeting the Japanese request.

Instead he decided once more for war. But he did not declare it immediately. He insisted on concluding what has been called a no-separate-peace treaty beforehand. He must have attached great importance to it, for he read and stressed the treaty prominently in his speech to the Reichstag. We may call this treaty the price to be paid by Japan for Germany's entering the war.

Viewed from this perspective and against the background

of his general considerations and the situation in December 1941, Hitler's decision becomes comprehensible. His failure to win a quick victory over Russia amounted to a failure of his concept of war in general. The war that he had envisioned as a series of lightning campaigns (*Blitzfeldzüge*) was now becoming a war of attrition just as the war of 1914–1918 had been. Then Russia had collapsed in the fourth year of the war and had had to accept the Treaty of Brest-Litovsk, with the result that Germany had gained immense lands in the east. Even so, in Hitler's view Germany had lost the war in the end for internal and external reasons, the latter referring to the American intervention, and he had since concentrated on overcoming these factors. The internal reasons had been removed by his racial policy. The external reasons were, as we have seen, Hitler's main concern in 1941.

It is a reasonable assumption that Hitler foresaw in December 1941 a development of the Second World War similar to that of the First: Russia could be defeated and America would intervene. But Germany did not have to lose the war if Japan took part in it. Japan could prevent America from all-out intervention in Europe by diverting that part of the American and British forces which so very narrowly had determined the outcome in 1918. In order to guarantee this sequence of events, Japan had to do more than enter the war. It had to be kept from pulling out before victory had been won in Europe. It had to be kept from concluding an early peace as it had done with other opponents in 1895 and 1905, in each instance in the second year of the war.

The treaty of December 11 to which Hitler attached so much importance, just like the earlier draft agreement of December 5, was to serve that precise purpose. In return for entering the war, Germany received the promise that Japan would not leave it. From Hitler's point of view this was not an unreasonable idea and there is no need to assume irrational motives. The declaration of war against the United States was an adequate step toward winning a war that essentially was and remained a war of conquest against the Soviet Union, in spite of the failure of the campaign of 1941. That war was madness, yet there was method in it.

5

Hitler and the Germans

Only rarely did Hitler and the Germans call each other by their proper names while they were contemporaries and made history together. Hitler usually did not address them as Germans, but as German folk comrades, and when he referred to them, he preferred to use the collective form and spoke of the German people or the German. He would say, for instance, that a German youth must be "as tough as leather and as hard as Krupp steel."[1] Or that "for the German soldier nothing is impossible."[2] The Germans, for their part, almost without exception called him the führer (even though they greeted each other with the phrase "Heil Hitler"), and the prescribed form of address was "my führer." The more intimate appellations applied to many statesmen were not at all commonly used, and it would have been unthinkable for a cheering crowd to shout "Adolf."

This seems to point to a rather impersonal relationship. But regardless of whether Hitler and the Germans loved each other or feared each other, what they thought of each other and, above all, how the one could emerge from the other are questions that can find their answers in a historical analysis.

Hitler always kept in mind what he had written in his book *Mein Kampf:* "The basic foundation for establishing authority is always popularity."[3] He immediately qualified that sentence and saw "in power . . . in force" the other principal basis of all authority.[4] Nevertheless, no saying of his has been handed down to posterity that even remotely resembles the words engraved on Napoleon's tomb: "May my ashes rest on the banks of the Seine near the people whom I loved so dearly." That Hitler loved the Germans is a dubious proposition; indeed he did not even want to be buried on the Spree, but in Linz on the Danube.[5]

Just as Alexander the Great was not a Greek, Napoleon not a Frenchman, and Stalin not a Russian, so Hitler came from the outside, at the least from outside the boundaries of the German national state created by Bismarck, and he spoke of the Germans in a distant manner, as if he didn't really belong to them. "Here too I am as cold as ice," he remarked during the war. "If the German people are not prepared to do battle for their self-preservation, then fine, let them perish!"[6] Even in public speeches he made these comments, as on December 18, 1940, to a group of officer candidates: "This nation will fade away" if it fails to assert its claim to existence.[7] Then "it should vanish," he declared to a foreign statesman on November 27, 1941.[8] Moreover he would "not shed a tear for it."[9] To be sure he wanted to make Germany great, greater than it had ever been in history. But he was less concerned with Germans as individuals—with their well-being and their fortunes—than with German blood, which he shed coldheartedly in order to expand the nation.

The Germans, by contrast, loved him rather than feared him. Even though we must verify the general truth of this statement and will indeed do so, this much is indisputable: Under Hitler the Germans never doubted, despaired, or revolted as they might have under a tyrant. Forces from abroad had to take him away from them, and only then was the spell that had bound them to each other for over twelve years broken, and it was broken immediately. Perhaps nothing characterizes the relationship of the Germans to Hitler so aptly as a phrase that was making the rounds in those days and went like this: "If only the führer knew about that!" Being applicable and indeed applied to the petty nuisances of daily life as well as to the great horrors of the regime, it absolved the führer (who after all could not concern himself with everything) of responsibility for specific events and also elevated him to the ranks of the unimpeachable.

One example can serve as evidence. When the mentally ill were being put to death by the tens of thousands at the beginning of the war, the district leader of a Nazi women's organization (certainly no enemy of the regime) wrote to the wife of the chief justice of the Nazi party on November 25, 1940: "People are still clinging to the hope that the führer knows nothing about these things, that he can't possibly know, otherwise he would stop them." And again, "The matter must be brought to the attention of the führer before it is too late and there must be a way for the voice of the German people to reach the ear of its führer."[10] A twofold deception! Naturally, Hitler knew what was to be brought to his attention. After all, it issued from his mouth and figured as his command. But far more important, the horrified reaction of the people not only reached him; he even listened to it, rescinded the order, and ended the operation.

In general, the relationship of the Germans to Hitler rested on deception, conscious deception on his part and self-deception on their part. He concealed his plans from them, although he knew exactly what he wanted, and they failed to recognize in him a causal agent even when he translated his intentions into action. They rewarded his deception with trust and, even under the worst circumstances, did not believe that they were being deceived but rather that he was being deceived.

In the beginning he had been open about his intentions. During the 1920s he repeatedly stated and wrote that a new war had to be waged in order to secure living space (*Lebensraum*) for Germany, and he had precisely articulated the domestic and foreign policy measures necessary to prepare the way. He had also repeatedly stated and written that the Jews had to be done away with, and he had noted that such a process was and would continue to be "a bloody one."[11] He had even mentioned poison gas in that context.[12] All this appeared in a book that had a distribution of hundreds of thousands of copies before 1933.

But it is also beyond doubt that the Germans did not grant him power in order to implement that program. Beginning with the memorable Reichstag elections of September 1930, when for the first time so many Germans voted for him that the chancellorship came within reach, Hitler deceived the Germans and the world. He had to remain silent about his war plans, if only to avoid alerting his adversaries. This, in turn, does not imply that the Germans themselves remained completely in the dark. That pluralistic party democracy was to be abolished and replaced by a rigid one-man rule was something the Germans well knew, and those who voted for Hitler favored that plan. That Hitler stood as an enemy to the Jews was something they also knew, put up with, or even condoned.

Hitler's rise to power may be controversial, but the numbers of Germans who voted for him is, by contrast, easy to determine. About every third German who went to the ballot box gave Hitler a vote at least once. One third—no more, no less. Even when he was in power, during the March elections of 1933 (which were no longer free yet still allowed alternatives), far more than half of all Germans did not vote for Hitler. How they viewed him after that can hardly be cap-

tured by statistics. From time to time public referendums were
held, but there was nothing to vote for between the register
of "yes" and "no." Even the officially announced electio
results, which very early recorded up to one-quarter "no
votes in some places, are unreliable, for falsification of ele
tion results is clearly documented in many cases.

But even when a nation is no longer polled, can no long
vote, and has lost the right to express opinions freely, pub
opinion still exists and can, within limits, be investigated.
Even a dictator—especially a dictator—is in his own interest eager to know what his subjects and above all his enemies
among those subjects think of him. Under Hitler, a kind of
comprehensive polling of public opinion arose from the police
surveillance and control of so-called ideological enemies and
was incorporated into an extensive set of reports. These
reports, which were collected and evaluated by several agencies but with especial zeal by the SD, the security department
of the party, tell us more about public moods than about
opinions. For the regime wanted above all to know whether
morale was good or bad. It was not disposed to heeding the
opinions of the populace; it intended to rule, and for that it
needed popularity, as Hitler himself had stated.

It goes without saying that the utmost care must be used in
drawing conclusions from reports on morale. Not that things
were glossed over in the reports; that would have made them
worthless. In the end they so dismayed the leadership that
Bormann prohibited them in the summer of 1944.[13] But there
is a certain arbitrariness inherent in them. Statistical evidence
of any precision is missing; reports often pertain only to certain parts of the Reich, and the spies did not, of course, find
out what people were afraid to say. The result is an impression, not a definitive conclusion; a portrait of moods, not of
opinions.

Generally speaking, one can say that morale fluctuated in a
peculiar way. It was lowered principally by the economic cares

of daily life, but then bolstered by foreign policy successes and later by military victories. Perhaps these responses were all too human, but still it seems to have been characteristic of this regime that it was more likely to win approval from the populace by diverting its attention from misery than by actually ameliorating conditions. Diversions of an intoxicating kind (presented in exactly that fashion) were abundantly available. Rarely has a generation been exposed to so many sensational new things in so few years.

The "Olympics, Spain, and the result of the London talks," states a report of August 1936, "are having a salutary effect on the morale of the populace and are helping us to smooth over all sorts of unpleasant things."[14] In the following year, when relatively little happened, morale evidently reached a low point. "A sense of discontent among the people is stronger than ever," stated a report of May 1937. "The National Socialist government is being held responsible for the shortage of raw materials."[15] The annexation of Austria then sparked "jubilation and joy." During the Sudeten crisis, "fear of war" reigned supreme, and after Munich there was once again "an elated mood."[16]

It is well know that the outbreak of war was greeted with little enthusiasm and with great apprehension. Nonetheless, a report on the events of June 1940 states that the victory in the west brought about "a degree of solidarity never hitherto achieved among the entire German people."[17] After this high point, things went slowly downhill again. The uncertainty of the course of the war, the increasing food shortages, and the air raids on German cities prompted a pessimistic mood that set in during the summer of 1942 and, after the battle of Stalingrad, shaded into doubt and resignation and finally into a still hopeful fatalism. The daily struggle for existence and survival displaced politics and dominated all other considerations. It should be noted, however, that the assassination attempt of July 20, 1944, was not only, with few exceptions, "unanimously" condemned but even contributed to a strengthening of the "bond to the führer."[18]

This, then, is in general the other predominant view, and with that we return to the fundamental issue: Whatever criticism may have been aired, Hitler was almost always spared it. Nearly every one of his speeches raised the general morale. People were disappointed if those speeches were not carried by the radio. They felt the need, as was reported during the war, "to hear, once again, the voice of the führer."[19] They wanted to see him too. A report of November 1940 stated, "we have almost reached the point where a newsreel without pictures of the führer is considered inferior. People always seem to want to see what the führer looks like, whether he appears serious or is laughing."[20] Similar sentiments were expressed even more emphatically in April 1943, when pictures of the führer had become rare. "A picture of the führer from which one could determine that, contrary to rumor, his hair had not turned completely white has a more positive effect on the mood of the people than a whole raft of battle slogans."[21]

Neither admiration, nor respect, nor even fear seems to characterize perfectly the attitude of the Germans toward Hitler. What they felt for him, especially during the war years, was an almost childlike devotion to a beloved father, a devotion that could easily dissolve into compassion. According to reports on morale, the general reaction to Rudolf Hess's flight to England was a "deeply felt sympathy . . . for the heavy blow that had struck the führer, 'who is not spared the cruel strokes of fate'."[22] Up to the very end, this reaction recurred whenever signs of defeat, disloyalty, or betrayal appeared—not least on July 20. "The führer is really spared nothing" was a phrase that functioned as a code word, much like the phrase "If only the führer knew about that!"

These observations do not correspond to what became the prevailing opinion after 1945, and the quotations cited above may therefore elicit indignant protest, especially among those who lived through those times. It is true that there was always dissent and even resistance: The reports on morale offer clear evidence of that. But it is also true, unfortunately, that this resistance (honorable and courageous though it was) receives an emphasis that may well be morally justified but that somewhat stretches the actual historical facts. When a German schoolbook dealt with National Socialism a few years ago under the rubric "Persecution and Resistance," that may well have been pedagogically salutary, but it did not represent the truth. On the other hand, this pessimistic view cannot and should not lead to a blanket moral condemnation of the Germans living at that time, for they were as a whole no worse and no better than the generations before and after them. But they were subjected to ordeals and to temptations that others escaped.

If one proceeds on the assumption that the Germans did not suddenly become criminals, then unusual circumstances must have led them to support the criminal that Hitler undoubtedly was. The nature of these circumstances is a significant question if we intend to go beyond superficial description to a historical analysis of the relationship of the German people to Hitler.

At the time of Hitler's rule, the vast majority of the German people were denied the kind of information that ordinarily builds the foundation of public opinion. Nothing shows this more clearly than the countless and often quite extravagant rumors that made the rounds in those days and were dutifully recorded in the reports on morale. Not infrequently those rumors had been put into circulation by Goebbels himself. The free expression of diverse opinions was replaced by a form of propaganda that twisted everything. Many fell victim to that propaganda out of sheer ignorance; those who voiced criticism publicly were persecuted by the police.

It must once again be emphasized that Hitler's rule over the

Germans did not in any way rest solely or even predominantly on the use of terror. That aspect of the regime has been too heavily stressed since 1945, for understandable reasons. Not even the crimes of the time can be explained in this way. Orders of a criminal nature were, as a rule, carried out not because of the threat of coercion, and rarely because people derived some kind of pleasure from committing a crime, but because of obedience, out of blindness, or for the sake of some advantage. Not one case is known in which a person's life was in danger or in which a person suffered serious consequences by refusing to participate in a crime, such as the murder of unarmed people. By the same token, membership in the Nazi party was a distinction that promised advantages and was thus not forced upon anyone, especially not on an unreliable person (a fact that is usually misunderstood or not mentioned these days); quite to the contrary, many people had their membership taken away from them. The party could in fact easily have had more members in the beginning than it actually had. Thus, the attitudes of the Germans under Hitler and to Hitler cannot be explained away by terror (except in the case of the persecuted).

Much more complicated and (for good reason) more controversial is the question concerning the circumstances that made Hitler's rule over the Germans possible. It would be easy to fill a book with nothing other than a list of the various explanations that have been proposed to date. The Versailles treaty and the Great Depression figure most prominently among them, but here too valid objections and refutations can be made. The Weimar Republic had almost succeeded in overcoming the financial impositions occasioned by the war before it collapsed, and the Great Depression hit the United States harder than it hit Germany, yet there it did not undermine democratic institutions. For a time a more literary approach to German history was very popular. Historians combed the writings of Bismarck and Frederick the Great and went back to Luther and even Arminius in their search for authoritarian predispositions in the German people, and both the romantic period and the Wilhelminian era yielded various interesting points.

Hard upon this analysis of intellectual currents came social and economic analysis. Capitalism, heavy industry, and the middle class were held responsible, and in recent years so-called theories of fascism (which have become ever more complicated) are held in high esteem. Yet at the same time there are also serious historians who, for well-founded reasons, attribute the rise of Hitler to the failings of individual figures. This business becomes completely hopeless when attempts are made to explain the origins of National Socialism through polemical allusions to one's own political or ideological adversaries. Such biased efforts are not only unscholarly but in most cases thoroughly contemptible.

The confusing array of serious explanations results not least from the fact that there is still no consensus on what exactly is to be explained; in other words, How should Hitler's rule be defined? For a long time, it had been viewed as a totalitarian or authoritarian dictatorship of great internal cohesiveness. But recently the many contradictory forces in it have received emphasis, for example, the so-called polycratic structures under which Hitler, in the final analysis, appears as a "weak dictator," a person driven by events rather than shaping them. Let us now review and reconsider the points discussed in earlier chapters.

A good description is, without doubt, the precondition for a good explanation. It is clearly insufficient simply to point to certain facts such as the Versailles treaty or the Great Depression, or even to intellectual currents. For there is no rational reason why such things should have led to Hitler's seizure of power and not, say, to a military dictatorship, a revolution, or to some altogether different phenomenon. The process deserves more careful investigation.

My explanation begins with the assumption that the regime that came to power in Germany in 1933 differed strikingly from the preceeding one and from earlier forms of government because it was a monocracy. For now we will take that to mean that all vital political decisions were made by one person, in this case Hitler. Yet this definition of the term is not really adequate. Military dictatorships are, in my view, not true monocracies, for the military dictator rules in conjunction with the military, and his power remains circumscribed by the extent to which the military is willing to support him. By the same token, monarchies, despite the linguistic contradiction, are also not necessarily monocracies of the kind meant here, especially in cases where the monarch depends on the nobility, derives his power from it, and is thereby also held in check by it.

Our monocrat, if I may put it in this way, rules in a vacuum as little as anyone else does. He too needs support. He does not receive it from one group alone but from several, which —and this is the decisive face—have entirely differing and even opposing interests, and also have differing and even opposing expectations about his rule. His power rests on being able to play these groups against each other. Every ruler does this to a certain degree while still remaining dependent on the factions supporting him. But for an autocrat, the support of different and opposing groups constitutes the actual source of his power.

These types of monocracies, which were probably described for the first time by Karl Marx and Friedrich Engels, may be rare in history, but they do occur. Examples in modern history are the absolute monarchies that played the various estates against each other, and the reigns of Napoleon I and Napoleon III, who maneuvered their way between the upper and lower bourgeoisie, or between the bourgeoisie and the workers. The special conditions under which such autocracies emerged have been convincingly analyzed in some cases, and it can be useful to draw upon such analyses as analogies for explaining Hitler's rise to power, assuming, of course, that he was actually a monocrat. Description and analysis thus go hand in hand.

As we have seen, Hitler came to power as the head of a coalition government. If the Nazi party had had a majority in the Reichstag, he would to a certain extent have been dependent on it. The support he received from his own following and from the Conservative party (two groups with wholly different interests) provided the preliminary basis for his monocracy. The creation of the government had not been guided by parliamentary procedure, if only because the two coalition partners together did not constitute a majority in the Reichstag. Moreover, this had been preceded by an intrigue in which the industrialist Wilhelm Keppler, then Hitler's economic adviser, had persuaded the banker Kurt von Schröder to arrange a conference between Hitler and Franz von Papen in Schröder's house in Cologne. The meeting took place on January 4, 1933, and the result was that Papen induced President Hindenburg to name Hitler chancellor of a coalition cabinet. We saw in chapter 1 that this story in reality is much more complicated than our brief summary. It passes over the motives of those participating in the intrigue, leaves open the question of whether they acted under instruction from specific groups, and says nothing about negotiations with other parties. Moreover, the intrigue of January 4 was of special importance, but it was not the only one of importance in those agitated weeks.

Again, we can briefly summarize what we have learned. Hitler did not come to power as the authorized representative of a specific group, but because of the support of several differing groups and persons who expected different things from the new chancellor. In that respect, his accession resembled a transfer of power rather than a seizure of power. The seizure of power and the establishment of monocracy took place when Hitler played the different groups supporting him against each other, as well as the groups that opposed him or stood on the sidelines. It was then that he revealed the distinctive nature of his regime. Once again, some briefly sketched examples must suffice.

Hitler flattered the conservatives by opening the new Reichstag in Potsdam and even led them to hope that he would restore the monarchy. At the same time, he promised work and bread to his followers, spoke of a "national revolution," yet shied away from tampering with property arrangements, although he allowed his private army, the SA, a free hand for the first anti-Jewish pogrom. He promised armament contracts to big business, new tasks to the army, protection to civil servants—in short, everything to everybody. On May 1, 1933, he gave the working classes the Labor Day holiday they had demanded in vain for decades; the next day he abolished the trade unions. In July he concluded a concordat with the Vatican and thereby put an end to the political power of the Center party. In September he bestowed on the farmers the Hereditary Estate Act, which guaranteed the unencumbered intergenerational transfer of small farms. On June 30, 1934, he sacrificed his party army, the SA, and thereby bound the regular army to him, but not without simultaneously strengthening his own police force, which then persecuted his remaining opponents.

Clearly Hitler was not the representative of any single group or class but of many groups at the same time. He served or threatened them all, giving something here and taking something there, always steering a middle course, even between the mutually hostile dental surgeons and dentists. He had no other choice if he wanted to stay in power, for no group was so powerful that he could base his power on it alone. His only hope was that the various factions would cripple each other.

Monocrats come to power through a stalemate, and this, as we have seen, is the fundamental fact, if not the decisive fact, about the Weimar Republic.

The stalemate appears on a superficial level in the contrast between the republicans and the supporters of the old regime. In parliamentary terms, the Weimar coalition, that is, the Social Democrats, the Democrats, and the Centrists, stood against a massive opposition force consisting of Conservatives and many former National Liberals, who either flatly rejected the new constitution or accepted it only grudgingly as an unfortunate fact of life. But is is only through the social structure that the contrast can be fully understood. On the one hand, there were those groups or classes that had served as the backbone of the old authoritarian state—those in large landed property and in business, the more prosperous bourgeoisie, the army, and the civil service. On the other hand there were those who had been excluded from the state and who had repeatedly been attacked as enemies of the state, that is, the working class and petit-bourgeois classes, which were constantly growing in the wake of industrialization.

In the upheaval surrounding the defeat of 1918, the former ruling class moved temporarily into the political opposition without losing its social and economic power. For property relations, the general economic order and even the state apparatus changed very little, if at all. That led to the unequal, or to be more accurate the equal, battle that characterized the political controversies in the Weimar Republic and increasingly assumed the character of a stalemate. One element in German society was no longer strong enough to control the government and the other element was not yet strong enough, indeed the less so since a third faction comprising the Communists and later the National Socialists proved itself incapable of forming a coalition either among themselves or, until 1933, with one of the other two factions.

This situation did not result simply from the lost war or

even the Versailles treaty. The main cause of the stalemate was a shift in the German social structure created primarily by the rise of the working class, whose growth had become politically manifest through the steady growth of the Socialists, which had furnished the strongest Reichstag delegation as early as 1912. The origins of this shift went back to the nineteenth century, long before the First World War led to the major problem of the inner structure of German society.

This problem suddenly erupted after the military collapse and led, with even greater bitterness, to the conflict that created the stalemate. That stalemate, in turn, found its most conspicuous expression in the breakup of the coalition of March 1930. Thereafter, no majority government whatever was formed, although that would have been perfectly possible given the distribution of power in the Reichstag. The majority were simply incapable of building a consensus, and the Republic thereby became parliamentarily ungovernable. Although we now know that the coalition government could have held out through the worst period of the Great Depression, the Reichstag was prematurely dissolved, and in the September elections of 1930 Hitler achieved his first great breakthrough. The numbers of his voters rose from 800,000 to 6.4 million, and those of his parliamentary representatives from 12 to 107. Hitler owed his victory to the inability of the Reichstag majority to build a consensus. This lack of consensus may have been triggered by problems related to the Great Depression, but it reflected a more fundamental failure of German society to reach a consensus.

Despite his victories, Hitler was by no means in power yet. He received more than twice as many votes in the Reichstag elections of July 1932 as he did in 1930, namely, 37.3 percent, but in the elections of November 1932, his percentage sank to 33.1 percent. Only after this defeat, in which two million voters deserted him or failed to return to the polls, did power come into his hands. He did not seize it, as he always

maintained and as many still hold today. Neither a parliamentary majority nor revolutionary force brought him to power.
Power was transferred to him through a confusing play of
forces. There was the formal designation by the Reich president, the coalition with the German Nationalists, and above
all the negotiations between public and private individuals.
These negotiations and the intrigue behind them could only
succeed because the parliamentary system was no longer func-
tioning, primarily because the constitutional parties had abdicated. The political decision-making process was thereby displaced to the realm of extraparliamentary affairs; the effect of
that displacement was to bestow on a wide array of forces a
freedom and influence that had not been foreseen in the constitution.

This was not a political development that saw the light of
day only in the last phase of the Weimar Republic. Since
neither of the two leading factions of German society dominated the government, a development took place that can be
described as the growing autonomy of the state apparatus.
Left without clear political directives, the army, the bureau-
cracy, and the judiciary for a long time had been acquiring
power of their own that expressed itself in actions of unprecedented arbitrariness. In the resulting power vacuum, officials
bound to accept direction freed themselves from control.

The fundamental state of the Republic bestowed, indeed
imposed, growing influence on generals and high officials as
well as on individual politicians and business leaders. Certainly they all had their own interests, as everyone does. But
one can also assume that they worried about a state that no
longer functioned properly. There was one fear that united all
the propertied classes, regardless of their differences of opinion in other matters, and that was their fear of a social revolution, of communism. The Communist party grew nonetheless. In the Reichstag elections of May 1928 it received 10.6
percent of the vote; in September 1930 13.1 percent; in July

1932 14.3 percent; in November 1932 16.9 percent. Its electoral share, unlike that of the Nazi party, did not decrease, and it preached expropriation and promised sovietization.

Hitler, on the other hand, gave reassuring promises and openly courted the industrialists. Whatever else one might have thought of him, he was certainly a passionate anticommunist. Moreover, he had at his disposal millions of largely poverty-stricken (and therefore dangerous) followers and possessed such a charismatic appeal for them that he seemed in a position to make them serve the state. It was true that he spoke without much restraint and that he intended to abolish the constitution. But had not this very constitution, an exceedingly unpopular one at that, led to the present dilemma? And was it not possible to control the risk of transferring power to him by taking him in, binding him to a coalition, fencing him in, and taming him?

This was the train of thought of the political powers in the winter of 1932-1933. However briefly the process has been described here, it nevertheless offers an explanation for Hitler's rise to power. Unable to exercise power in their own right, the property holders of Germany, led by industrialists such as Keppler, bankers such as Schröder, and conservative politicians such as Papen, secured political power for a charismatic hero of the masses in the hope that he would at least protect their economic power and ward off a social revolution. To put it concisely, this constituted a pact with the devil: political power for economic stability. One was sacrificed to secure the other. And this plan did not, after all, fail completely, even though catastrophes of unimaginable extent followed and in the end buried the state.

Hitler could rule as he wanted so long as he did not seriously antagonize any of the differing and opposing factions that had helped him rise to power, neither his indigent followers nor his propertied stirrup holders, nor any of the other great social forces (such as the churches) whose institutions he was not in a position to destroy. This was the hallmark of his monocracy, its strength as well as its weakness, and Hitler fully understood his position. He was always haunted by the fear of being pushed off the throne.

There is much to be said for the view that Hitler, like the two Napoleons, turned to foreign adventures in order to preserve his political power. The way in which he ran state finances essentially allowed only a choice between bankruptcy or war. On the other hand, his foreign policy was not improvised, but followed a rigid plan that Hitler had designed long before coming to power and had incorporated into his world view. This plan, furthermore, was not wholly incongruent with general developments and its realization was therefore ensured. Late imperialistic territorial conquest was presaged in the development of Germany, just as it was in the development of Japan and Italy. All three states had entered world politics at the same time, around 1870, met disappointment in the result of World War I, and allied themselves subsequently. Thus Hitler, notwithstanding his own great personal responsibility in shaping events, was no more than the executer of a longstanding tendency.

With the accession of Hitler, however, German society had deprived itself of the opportunity to determine, according to its own interests, whether and how the path inherent in its development was to be taken. There were attempts, above all through military resistance, to prevent Hitler from taking the path to war or at least to complete defeat. Nevertheless, neither the military nor any other group that had made Hitler's accession possible was strong enough to win back its power of co-determination once it had abdicated it. Hitler led them all, up to the bitter end, to the destruction of their state.

The most horrifying thing is also the most difficult to explain: the murder of the Jews and of the often forgotten gypsies. Here too Hitler's personal responsibility was great.

Certainly, there are convincing answers to the question why minorities are persecuted. During a crisis, the majority often sees in them the guilt that it cannot recognize in itself or in the circumstances. But this wasn't even, in the final analysis, a gigantic pogrom. The vast bureaucratic process of a cold-bloodedly organized and mechanized mass murder—one without historical precedent—simply cannot be attributed to the kind of atmosphere that led to pogroms, much as that might explain what happened. The rational power of language becomes paralyzed in the face of that event.

Our historical analysis of Hitler and the Germans may perhaps sound more rational than the subject would warrant. Even the sober historian who becomes absorbed in the attempt to understand the past knows that there are more things in heaven and earth than are dreamt of in his philosophy. He also knows that he can count on more applause if he tags the guilty with some weighty value judgments. It is easy enough to name crooks and criminals; they are, moreover, palpable and especially visible after the fact. Yet they have also always existed and will continue to exist. The task of scholarship is therefore to try to explain why they sometimes exist on the fringes of society, and sometimes stand at its very center.

The Germans have been liberated from Hitler, yet they will never be free of him. He himself will never return, and even the danger of another monocracy like his is remote in view of current social developments. That quite peculiar constellation of circumstances that made his rule possible cannot, in my view, recur within the foreseeable future. What other dangers threaten us is a question that cannot be addressed in this context. But it is important to note that even the dead Hitler will always remain with the Germans, with the survivors, with their descendants, and even with the unborn. He will be with them, not as he was with his contemporaries, but as an eternal monument to what is humanly possible.

Notes

CHAPTER I

Bibliographical Note
   The preceding essay represents a continuation of three earlier articles. Although partly out of date, these articles deserve mention because they cover issues that I cannot address again here. The first describes above all what my interpretation owes to the path-breaking writings of Karl Marx and Friedrich Engels.
   Jäckel, Eberhard. "Wie kam Hitler an die Macht?" In Karl Dietrich Erdmann and Hagen Schulze (eds.), *Selbstpreisgabe einer Demokratie.* Düsseldorf, 1980.
   ————. "Hitler und die Deutschen." In *Hitlers Weltanschauung. Erweiterte und überarbeitete Neuausgabe.* Stuttgart, 1981.
   ————. "Der Machtantritt Hitlers—Versuch einer geschichtlichen Erklärung." In Volker Rittberger (ed.), *1933: Wie die Republik der Diktatur erlag.* Stuttgart, 1983.
   The following is an alphabetical list of the most important studies on which I have drawn.
   Bracher, Karl Dietrich. *Die Auflösung der Weimarer Republik.* 1955. Königstein, 1978.
   ————. *Die nationalsozialistische Machtergreifung.* Cologne, 1960.
   Dorpalen, Andreas. *Hindenburg in der Geschichte der Weimarer Republik.* Berlin, 1966.
   Eschenburg, Theodor. *Die improvisierte Demokratie.* Munich, 1963.
   Hamilton, Richard F. *Who Voted for Hitler?* Princeton, N.J., 1982.
   Hubatsch, Walter (ed.). *Hindenburg und der Staat.* Göttingen, 1966.
   Huber, Ernst Rudolf. *Deutsche Verfassungsgeschichte seit 1789.* Vol. 6, *Die Weimarer Reichsverfassung.* Stuttgart, 1981.
   Kershaw, Ian. *Der Hitler-Mythos.* Stuttgart, 1980.
   Kuhn, Axel. "Die Unterredung zwischen Hitler und Papen im Hause des Barons von Schröder. *Geschichte in Wissenschaft und Unterricht 24* (1973): 709ff.
   Merkl, Peter H. *Political Violence under the Swastika: 581 Early Nazis.* Princeton, N.J., 1975.
   Milatz, Alfred. *Wähler und Wahlen in der Weimarer Republik.* Bonn, 1965.
   Neebe, Reinhard. *Großindustrie, Staat und NSDAP 1930–1933.* Göttingen, 1981.

108   **Notes**

Passchier, Nico. "The Electoral Geography of the Nazi Landslide." In Stein Ugelvik Larsen et al. (eds.) *Who Were the Fascists.* Bergen, 1980.

Schulze, Hagen. *Weimar: Deutschland 1917–1933.* Berlin, 1982.

Stachura, Peter D. (ed.). *The Shaping of the Nazi State.* London, 1978.

Turner, Henry Ashby, Jr. *Faschismus und Kapitalismus in Deutschland: Studien zum Verhältnis zwischen Nationalsozialismus und Wirtschaft.* Göttingen, 1972.

———. "Das Verhältnis des Großunternehmertums zur NSDAP." In Hans Mommsen et al. (ed.). *Industrielles System und politische Entwicklung in der Weimarer Republik.* Düsseldorf, 1974.

———. "Großunternehmertum und Nationalsozialismus 1930–1933." *Historische Zeitschrift* 221 (1975): 18ff.

———. "Hitlers Einstellung zu Wirtschaft und Gesellschaft vor 1933." *Geschichte und Gesellschaft* 2 (1976): 89ff.

Vogelsang, Thilo. *Reichswehr, Staat und NSDAP.* Stuttgart, 1962.

Weber, Hermann (ed.). *Die Generallinie: Rundschreiben des Zentralkomitees der KPD an die Bezirke 1929–1933.* Düsseldorf, 1981.

Weßling, Wolfgang. "Hindenburg, Neudeck und die deutsche Wirtschaft." *Vierteljahrsschrift für Sozial- und Wirtschaftsgeschichte* 64 (1977): 41ff.

Wheeler-Bennett, John W. *Der hölzerne Titan: Paul von Hindenburg.* Tübingen, 1969.

1. The most recent and detailed explication of the constitutional aspects is by Ernst Rudolf Huber in *Deutsche Verfassungsgeschichte seit 1789,* vol. 6, *Die Weimarer Reichsverfassung* (Stuttgart: Kohlhammer, 1981). The relevant documents are published in his *Dokumente zur deutschen Verfassungsgeschichte,* vol. 3, *Dokumente der Novemberrevolution und der Weimarer Republik 1918–1933* (Stuttgart: Kohlhammer, 1966).

2. Andreas Dorpalen. *Hindenburg and the Weimar Republic* (Princeton, N.J., 1964). I have used the German translation: *Hindenburg in der Geschichte der Weimarer Republik,* trans. Charlotte Dixon and Margarete von Eynern (Berlin: Leber, 1966), p. 409.

3. See Helga Timm, *Die deutsche Sozialpolitik und der Bruch der grossen Koalition im März 1930* (1952; Reprint Düsseldorf: Droste, 1982).

4. See the important works by Henry Ashby Turner, Jr., listed in the Bibliographical Note.

CHAPTER 2

1. Eberhard Jäckel, *Hitlers Weltanschauung,* enlarged and revised ed., (Stuttgart: Deutsche Verlags-Anstalt, 1981). An English translation was published under the title *Hitler's Weltanschauung* (Middletown, Conn.:

Wesleyan University Press, 1972) and reprinted as *Hitler's World View* (Cambridge, Mass.: Harvard University Press, 1981). It should be noted that the two English books are identical and based upon the first German edition. The second German edition made use of new material published in Eberhard Jäckel and Axel Kuhn (eds.), *Hitler: Sämtliche Aufzeichnungen 1905-1924* (Stuttgart: Deutsche Verlags-Anstalt, 1980).

2. See Wolfgang Wippermann, *Die Bonapartismustheorie von Marx und Engels* (Stuttgart: Klett-Cotta, 1983).

3. A good selection of materials on this subject may be found in Gerhard Hirschfeld et al. (eds.)., *Der "Führerstaat": Mythos and Realität* (Stuttgart: Klett-Cotta, 1981); see particularly the essays by Tim Mason and Hans Mommsen.

4. Ernst Rudolf Huber, *Verfassungsrecht des Grossdeutschen Reiches* (Hamburg, 1939), p. 160.

5. Hans Mommsen, "Nationalsozialismus," in C. D. Kernig (ed.), *Sowjetsystem und Demokratische Gesellschaft*, vol. 4 (Freiburg: Herder, 1971), p. 702.

6. See Harold C. Deutsch, *Hitler and His Generals: The Hidden Crisis, January–June 1938* (Minneapolis: University of Minnesota Press, 1974).

7. See Klaus-Jürgen Müller, *General Ludwig Beck* (Boppard: Boldt, 1980).

8. Marlis G. Steinert, *Hitlers Krieg und die Deutschen* (Düsseldorf: Econ, 1970), p. 156.

9. Generaloberst Halder, *Kriegstagebuch*, vol. 2 (Stuttgart: Kohlhammer, 1963). p. 49.

10. Hans-Adolf Jacobsen, "Kommissarbefehl und Massenexekutionen sowjetischer Kriegsgefangener," in Hans Buchheim et al. (eds.), *Anatomie des SS-Staates*, vol. 2 (Olten: Walter, 1965).

11. Nuremberg Document L-221, *Der Prozess gegen die Hauptkriegsverbrecher vor dem Internationalen Militärgerichtshof*, vol. 38 (Nuremberg, 1949), p. 88 (hereafter cited as IMT).

12. Notes by General Liebmann, published in *Vierteljahrshefte für Zeitgeschichte* 2 (1954): 435.

13. Nuremberg Document PS-386, *IMT*, vol. 25, pp. 402ff.

14. Adolf Hitler, *Mein Kampf*, vol. 2 (Munich: Eher, 1927; reprint 1930), p. 579.

15. See Bernd Wegner, *Hitlers Politische Soldaten: Die Waffen-SS 1933–1945* (Paderborn: Schöningh, 1982).

16. Helmut Heiber (ed.), *Hitlers Lagebesprechungen* (Stuttgart: Deutsche Verlags-Anstalt, 1962), pp. 63ff.

17. Ernest Fraenkel, *The Dual State* (New York: Oxford University Press, 1940).

18. Winston S. Churchill, *The Second World War*, vol. 1 (London: Cassell, 1948), p. ix.

CHAPTER 3

1. The two principal comprehensive works still are Gerald Reitlinger, *The Final Solution* (London: Valentine, 1953), and Raul Hilberg, *The Destruction of the European Jews* (Chicago: Quadrangle, 1961).
2. Christopher R. Browning, "The Decision concerning the Final Solution" (unpublished lecture, Paris, 1982).
3. Martin Broszat, "Hitler und die Genesis der 'Endlösung'," *Vierteljahrshefte für Zeitgeschichte* 25 (1977): 739–775. See Christopher R. Browning's reply, "Zur Genesis der 'Endlösung'," ibid. 29 (1981): 97–109. An English translation of Broszat's article is available in *Yad Vashem Studies* (1979), Vol. 13, pp. 61–98. The most recent functionalist interpretation is Hans Mommsen, "Die Realisierung des Utopischen: Die 'Endlösung der Judenfrage' im 'Dritten Reich'" *Geschichte und Gesellschaft* 9 (1983): 381–420.
4. For more details see my book *Hitlers Weltanschauung*. (Stuttgart: Deutsche Verlags-Anstalt, 1981).
5. Eberhard Jäckel and Axel Kuhn (eds.), *Hitler: Sämtliche Aufzeichnungen 1905–1924* (Stuttgart: Deutsche Verlags-Anstalt, 1980), pp. 88-90.
6. Adolf Hitler, *Mein Kampf*, vol. 2 (Munich: Eher, 1927; reprint, 1930), p. 738.
7. Ibid., p. 772.
8. Jäckel and Kuhn, *Hitler,* p. 280.
9. Gerhard L. Weinberg (ed.), *Hitlers Zweites Buch* (Stuttgart: Deutsche Verlags-Anstalt, 1961); English translation: *Hitler's Secret Book* (New York: Grove Press, 1964).
10. *Akten zur deutschen auswärtigen Politik 1918–1945, Serie D: 1937–1941*, vol. 12, 2, p. 838 (hereafter cited as *ADAP*).
11. Hugh R. Trevor-Roper (ed.), *Hitler's Table Talk, 1941–1944* (London: Weidenfeld, 1953), p. 79.
12. Rudolph Binion, "'Der Jude ist weg': Machtpolitische Auswirkungen des Hitlerschen Rassengedankens," in Josef Becker et al. (eds.), *Die Deutsche Frage im 19. und 20. Jahrhundert* (Munich: Vögel, 1983), pp. 347–372. See also Binion's earlier work, *Hitler among the Germans* (New York: Elsevier, 1976).
13. Lecture in Hamburg, March 23, 1938. Max Domarus (ed.), *Hitler: Reden und Proklamationen 1932–1945*, 2 vols. (Neustadt a.d. Aisch: Schmidt, 1962 and 1963), p. 839 (hereafter cited as Domarus).
14. June 6, 1938. *Droste Geschichts-Kalendarium*, vol. 2, 1 (Düsseldorf: Droste, 1982), p. 451.
15. Conference, October 14, 1938. Nuremberg Document PS-1301, *Der Prozess gegen die Hauptkriegsverbrecher vor dem Internationalen Militärgerichtshof*, vol. 27 (Nuremberg, 1948), p. 163 (hereafter cited as *IMT*).
16. *ADAP*, vol. 5, nos. 84, 88, 89, 91, 92, 95, 97, 98, 101, 103, 107, 127, 652, 664, 665.

17. Conference, November 12, 1938. Nuremberg Document PS−1816, *IMT,* vol. 28, pp. 538−539.

18. *ADAP,* vol. 4, p. 293.

19. Helmut Krausnick, "Judenverfolgung," in Hans Buchheim et al. (eds.), *Anatomie des SS-Staates,* vol. 2 (Olten: Walter, 1965), p. 338.

20. *ADAP,* vol. 4, p. 170.

21. Krausnick, "Judenverfolgung," pp. 342−343.

22. *Stenographische Berichte des Reichstags* (1939), p. 16(B).

23. Jochen Thies, *Architekt der Weltherrschaft* (Düsseldorf: Droste, 1976), p. 115.

24. Krausnick, "Judenverfolgung," p. 351.

25. Hans-Günther Seraphim (ed.), *Das politische Tagebuch Alfred Rosenbergs* (Munich: Deutscher Taschenbuch Verlag, 1964), p. 99.

26. Nuremberg Document PS-686, *IMT,* vol. 26, pp. 255−257. Cf. Robert L. Koehl, *RKFDV: German Resettlement and Population Policy 1939−1945* (Cambridge, Mass.: Harvard University Press, 1957).

27. Werner Präg and Wolfgang Jacobmeyer (eds.), *Das Diensttagebuch des deutschen Generalgouverneurs in Polen 1939 − 1945* (Stuttgart: Deutsche Verlags-Anstalt, 1975), pp. (hereafter cited as *Diensttagebuch*).

28. Reitlinger, *The Final Solution,* p. 46.

29. To Colin Ross, March 12, 1940, *ADAP,* vol. 8, p. 716.

30. "Denkschrift Himmlers über die Behandlung der Fremdvölkischen im Osten (Mai 1940)," *Vierteljahrshefte für Zeitgeschichte* 5 (1957): 197.

31. Krausnick, "Judenverfolgung," p. 355.

32. See Eberhard Jäckel, *Frankreich in Hitlers Europa* (Stuttgart: Deutsche Verlags-Anstalt, 1966), pp. 46−58.

33. Paul Schmidt, *Statist auf diplomatischer Bühne 1923−45* (Bonn: Athenäum, 1952), p. 485.

34. *Diensttagebuch,* p. 252.

35. Jäckel, *Frankreich,* pp. 81 and 128−129.

36. *Diensttagebuch,* p. 284.

37. Ibid., p. 327.

38. Letter from Lammers to Schirach, December 3, 1940, Nuremberg Document PS-1950, *IMT,* vol 29, p. 176.

39. Krausnick, "Judenverfolgung," p. 358.

40. *Diensttagebuch,* pp. 335-337.

41. See Helmut Krausnick and Hans-Heinrich Wilhelm, *Die Truppe des Weltanschauungskrieges: Die Einsatzgruppen der Sicherheitspolizei und des SD, 1938−1942* (Stuttgart: Deutsche Verlags-Anstalt, 1981).

42. Krausnick, "Judenverfolgung," p. 371.

43. Reitlinger, *The Final Solution,* p. 28.

44. *Diensttagebuch,* p. 336.

45. Ibid., p. 386.

46. For example, in a letter of July 5, 1943, Himmler called Sobibór a *Durchgangslager,* as did other SS officials in the ensuing correspondence. Adalbert Rückerl (ed.), *Nationalsozialistische Vernichtungslager* (Munich:

Deutscher Taschenbuch Verlag, 1977), pp. 176–178.
47. To Marshal Kvaternik, *ADAP,* vol. 13, 2, p. 838.
48. Alfred Streim, *Die Behandlung sowjetischer Kriegsgefangener im "Fall Barbarossa"* (Heidelberg: C. F. Müller, 1981), pp. 74–93.
49. Józef Marszalek, *Majdanek* (Reinbek bei Hamburg: Rowohlt, 1982), pp. 24–26.
50. *Diensttagebuch,* p. 389.
51. See Yisrael Gutman, *The Jews of Warsaw, 1939–1943* (Brighton: Harvester Press, 1982), and Raul Hilberg et al. (eds.), *The Warsaw Diary of Adam Czerniakow* (New York: Stein and Day, 1979).
52. Nuremberg Document PS-710, *IMT,* vol. 26, pp. 266–267. That the authorization was prepared by Heydrich in advance and was written by Eichmann: Rudolf Aschenauer (ed.), *Ich, Adolf Eichmann* (Leoni: Druffel, 1980), p. 479. That Heydrich went to see Göring is confirmed by an entry in Göring's appointment book: *Vierteljahrshefte für Zeitgeschichte* 31 (1983): 366–367.
53. Goebbels diary, August 20, 1941, quoted by Broszat, "Hitler," p. 750.
54. See Martin Broszat (ed.), *Kommandant in Auschwitz: Autobiographische Aufzeichnungen von Rudolf Höss* (Stuttgart: Deutsche Verlags-Anstalt, 1958), p. 153, and Jochen von Lang (ed.), *Das Eichmann-Protokoll* (Berlin: Severin und Siedler, 1982), p. 69.
55. Hans-Heinrich Wilhelm, "Wie geheim war die 'Endlösung'?," in *Miscellanea: Festschrift für Helmut Krausnick* (Stuttgart: Deutsche Verlags-Anstalt, 1980), p. 137.
56. Robert M. W. Kempner, *Eichmann und Komplizen* (Zürich: Europa Verlag, 1961), p. 87.
57. Note by Rosenberg, Nuremberg Document PS-1517, *IMT,* vol. 27, p. 270.
58. Nuremberg Document PS-709, published in Rückerl, *Nationalsozialistische Vernichtungslager,* pp. 99–100.
59. Document 203 AR 690/65, Zentrale Stelle der Landesjustizverwaltungen, Ludwigsburg; quoted by Broszat, "Hitler," p. 749. On SS-Sturmbannführer Rolf-Heinz Höppner, who signed the letter, see Martin Pollack, "Jäger und Gejagter," *Transatlantik,* November 1982, pp. 17–24.
60. Bradley F. Smith and Agnes F. Peterson (eds.), *Heinrich Himmler: Geheimreden 1933 bis 1945* (Berlin: Propyläen, 1974), pp. 169 (Oct. 6, 1943), 202 (May 5, 1944), 203 (May 24, 1944), and 203–204 (June 21, 1944).
61. Louis P. Lochner (ed.), *Goebbels Tagebücher aus den Jahren 1942–43* (Zürich: Atlantis, 1948), pp. 142–143.
62. Kempner, *Eichmann,* p. 97.
63. *Vierteljahrshefte für Zeitgeschichte* 11 (1963): 206–209.
64. Browning, "Decision" (see note 2).
65. Broszat, "Hitler," p. 764.
66. Helmut Heiber, "Aus den Akten des Gauleiters Kube, *Vierteljahr-*

shefte für Zeitgeschichte 4 (1956): 67–92.

67. Seev Goshen, "Eichmann und die Nisko-Aktion im Oktober 1939," *Vierteljahrshefte für Zeitgeschichte* 29 (1981): 74–96.

68. Keesings Archiv der Gegenwart 1942, p. 5705.

69. Adolf Hitler, *Hitlers Politisches Testament: Die Bormann Diktate vom Februar und April 1945* (Hamburg: Knaus, 1981), pp. 70 and 122.

70. Felix Kersten, *Klerk en beul* (Amsterdam: Meulenhoff, 1948), p. 198.

CHAPTER 4

This chapter is a revised version of an essay originally published under the title "Die deutsche Kriegserklärung an die Vereinigten Staaten von 1941," in *Im Dienste Deutschlands und des Rechts: Festschrift für Wilhelm G. Grewe* (Baden-Baden: Nomos, 1981), pp. 117–137.

1. *Akten zur deutschen auswärtigen Politik 1918–1945, Serie D. 1937–1941,* vol. 13, 2, pp. 817 and 812–813 (hereafter cited as *ADAP*).

2. Max Domarus (ed.), *Hitler: Reden und Proklamationen 1932–1945,* 2 vols. (Neustadt a.d. Aisch: Schmidt, 1962 and 1963), pp. 1794–1811.

3. *ADAP*, vol. 13, 2, p. 813.

4. See once more my book *Hitlers Weltanschauung* (Stuttgart: Deutsche Verlags-Anstalt, 1981), and Axel Kuhn, *Hitlers aussenpolitisches Programm* (Stuttgart: Klett, 1970).

5. *ADAP*, vol. 11, 1, pp. 175–176.

6. Hans-Adolf Jacobsen (ed.), *Kriegstagebuch des Oberkommandos der Wehrmacht,* vol. 1 (Frankfurt am Main: Bernard and Graefe, 1965), p. 328.

7. Walther Hubatsch (ed.), *Hitlers Weisungen für die Kriegführung 1939–1945* (Frankfurt am Main: Bernard und Graefe, 1962), pp. 103–104.

8. See Peter Herde, *Pearl Harbor* (Darmstadt: Wissenschaftliche Buchgesellschaft, 1980).

9. *ADAP*, vol. 12, 1, pp. 317–324 and 374–378.

10. *Foreign Relations of the United States, Diplomatic Papers,* vol. 4, *The Far East* (Washington, D.C., 1956), p. 933.

11. Andreas Hillgruber, "Japan und der Fall 'Barbarossa': Japanische Dokumente zu den Gesprächen Hitlers und Ribbentrops mit Botschafter Oshima von Februar bis Juni 1941, *Wehrwissenschaftliche Rundschau* 18 (1968): 312–335.

12. Leonidas E. Hill (ed.), *Die Weizsäcker-Papiere 1933–1950* (Berlin: Propyläen, 1974), p. 258.

13. Gerhard Wagner (ed.), *Lagevorträge des Oberbefehlshabers der Kriegsmarine vor Hitler 1939–1945* (Frankfurt am Main: Bernard und Graefe, 1972), p. 263.

14. Nobutaka Ike (ed.), *Japan's Decision for War: Records of the 1941 Policy Conferences* (Stanford, Calif.: Stanford University Press, 1967), p. 60.

15. *ADAP*, vol. 13, 1, p. 34.

16. Wagner, *Lagevorträge*, pp. 264–265.
17. *ADAP*, vol. 13, 1, p. 95.
18. ADAP, vol. 13, 2, p. 834.
19. Wagner, *Lagevorträge*, p. 286.
20. Genraloberst Halder, *Kriegstagebuch,* vol. 3 (Stuttgart: Kohlhammer, 1964), p. 219.
21. *ADAP*, vol. 13, 1, p. 413.
22. *ADAP*, vol. 13, 2, pp. 497 and 499.
23. Ibid., p. 547.
24. Ibid., p. 586.
25. Ibid., pp. 653 and 610 n. 4.
26. Ibid., p. 653.
27. Ibid., p. 660.
28. Ibid., p. 665.
29. Ike, *Japan's Decision for War,* pp. 241–242.
30. Department of Defense, *The "Magic" Background of Pearl Harbor,* vol. 4 (Washington, D.C.: U.S. Government Printing Office, 1978). See also Peter Herde, *Italien, Deutschland und der Weg in den Krieg im Pazifik 1941* (Wiesbaden: Steiner, 1983), where the Italian documents are used as well.
31. *ADAP*, vol. 13, 2, pp. 708–710.
32. Department of Defense, *The "Magic" Background,* p. A-383.
33. Ibid., p. A-388.
34. This is evident from several sources. See Guenther Blumentritt, *Von Rundstedt: The Soldier and the Man* (London: Odhams, 1952), p. 114.
35. Domarus, *Hitler: Reden und Proklamationen,* p. 1788.
36. Department of Defense, *The "Magic" Background,* p. A-389.
37. *ADAP*, vol. 13, 2, pp. 781–783.
38. Ibid., pp. 779–780.
39. Ibid., p. 781.
40. Hill, *Die Weizsäcker-Papiere,* pp. 278–279.
41. *ADAP*, vol. 13, 2, pp. 799–800.
42. Domarus, *Hitler: Reden und Proklamationen,* p. 1793.
43. Wagner, *Lagevorträge,* p. 327.
44. *ADAP*, vol. 13, 2, pp. 807–812.
45. Ibid., pp. 812–813.
46. Its official title, as published in the *Reichsgesetzblatt* of February 13, 1942, was "Abkommen zwischen Deutschland, Italien und Japan über die gemeinsame Kriegführung gegen die Vereinigten Staaten und England."
47. Hill, *Die Weizsäcker-Papiere,* p. 274.

CHAPTER 5

This chapter was originally a lecture and was later included in the second edition of my *Hitlers Weltanschauung* (Stuttgart: Deutsche Verlags-Anstalt, 1981).

1. Speech of September 14, 1935, at Nuremberg. Max Domarus (ed.), *Hitler: Reden und Proklamationen 1932–1945*, 2 vols. (Neustadt a.d. Aisch: Schmidt, 1962 and 1963), p. 533.

2. Speech of May 4, 1941, before the Reichstag. Domarus, p. 1704.

3. Adolf Hitler, *Mein Kampf*, vol. 2 (Munich: Eher, 1927); reprint 1930), p. 579.

4. Ibid.

5. Albert Speer, *Erinnerungen* (Berlin: Propyläen, 1969), p. 113. In an earlier will Hitler had wished to be buried in Munich; see Gerhard L. Weinberg, "Hitler's Private Testament of May 2, 1938," *Journal of Modern History* (1955): 415–419.

6. Adolf Hitler, *Monologe im Führerhauptquartier 1941–1944* (Hamburg: Knaus, 1980), p. 239.

7. Domarus, p. 1639.

8. *Akten zur deutschen auswärtigen Politik 1918–1945, Serie D: 1937–1941*, vol. 13, 2, p. 705.

9. Ibid., p. 708.

10. Marlis G. Steinert, *Hitlers Krieg und die Deutschen* (Düsseldorf: Econ, 1970), p. 156.

11. Hitler, *Mein Kampf*, p. 738.

12. Ibid., p. 772.

13. Heinz Boberach (ed.), *Meldungen aus dem Reich* (Neuwied: Luchterhand, 1965), pp. XXVII–XXVIII.

14. Steinert, pp. 76–77.

15. Ibid., p. 62.

16. Ibid., pp. 77–79.

17. Boberach, p. 77.

18. Steinert, pp. 469-490.

19. Boberach, p. 191.

20. Ibid., p. 116.

21. Ibid., p. 384.

22. Ibid., p. 146.